W.O.R.K.

Wonderful **O**pportunities
for Raising
Responsible **K**ids

W.O.R.K.

Wonderful **O**pportunities
for Raising
Responsible **K**ids

By Debbie Bowen

Second Printing: July, 2004
2 e.

International Standard Book Number:
0-88290-755-7

Horizon Publishers' Catalog and Order Number:
H1984

Printed and distributed
in the United States of America by CFI

925 North Main
Springville, Utah 84663

Local Phone: (801) 489-4084
Toll Free: 1 (800) skybook
FAX: (801) 489-1097

E-mail: skybook@www.cedarfort.com
Website: http://www.cedarfort.com

Contents

What Readers Have Said About This Book

Debbie Bowen's kid-tested philosophies have completely changed my paradigm about getting children to work and to take responsibility in the home. Her suggestions are insightful, practical, and amazingly effective.

—Maria Covey Cole, mother of five

Debbie Bowen's book, *W.O.R.K.,* encouraged and motivated me through her true-to-life personal experiences. The specifics on teaching children the "What, Why, and How" when delegating chores made a difference in our home the very next day!

—Ann Jarvis Passey, mother of six

The ideas in this book work. How else could this mother of ten have time to write it? I just wish I had time to read it before my children were grown. It's definitely one I'm going to share with others.

—Ann Allred, mother of five

Teaching our children to work without complaint is something of a holy grail in our house. Productive children are happy children. Children who know the joy of a job well done are well equipped for success. I've looked through many a parenting shelf in bookstores across the country and Debbie Bowen's book *W.O.R.K.* is quite simply the most thoughtful, practical, and helpful discussion of this vital topic that I've found. These principles have changed the dynamic in our home.

—Timothy Robinson, father of four

Labor is life.
—Thomas Carlyle

Man must work.
There is no work so rude that he may not exalt it;
no work so impassive that he may not breathe a soul into it;
no work so dull that he may not enliven it.
—Henry Giles

Acknowledgments

I would like to thank everyone who has had part in the success of this book:

The many friends and family who have provided encouragement and expressed interest in this book while it was in the making.

Timothy Robinson who saw the book's potential when it was far from finished. His suggestions regarding content, style, and structure improved the book dramatically.

Horizon Publishers for getting this book printed in record time. They truly went the extra mile, and I am most grateful for the efforts of all those involved.

My parents, Bob and Susie Gilham, who are some of the hardest working people I know and who instilled in me a love for and an understanding of the value of work.

My husband, Bruce, who is my greatest source of encouragement and support, who has spent countless hours tending the children so I could have quiet writing time, and who is my friend and companion in the never-ending struggle of teaching our children to work.

And, of course, my children—Trenton, Jadee, Caleb, Camille, Isaac, Jarom, Abram, Levi, Melia, and Marissa—without whom there would have been no book to write! I appreciate their help and cooperation in our daily toils.

Front: Isaac, Jadee, Bruce, Camille
Back: Caleb, Marissa, Abram, Debbie, Melia, Jarom, Trenton
Top: Levi

Preface
OUR FAMILY PHILOSOPHY

Love, therefore, labor; It is wholesome to the
body and good for the mind.—William Penn

By worldly standards, we were never rich. Dad was a school
teacher and Mom was a homemaker. Consequently, we didn't
have much money, we didn't go on many vacations, and we
didn't own expensive play toys. Yet, somehow we never felt
disadvantaged. We were rich in other ways. My mother, a
daughter of German immigrants, and my father, of Native
American descent who spent his teenage years on the Reserva-
tion, knew firsthand the value of perseverance and self-reliance in
making something of themselves; and they passed on to their five
children a legacy of thrift and industry. There was meaning and
substance to our lives that could not be purchased with money.

We grew up in a small farming community with acres of alfalfa, corn, and sugar beets. Home was a quiet neighborhood at the
end of a dead-end street surrounded by an empty field, a small
farm with a barn and pastures for horses, and neighbors with large
lots on which they grew impressive gardens. It was a happy childhood full of many pleasant memories: making houses in the nearby field by trampling down the alfalfa; late night yard games with
the neighborhood children; fresh vegetables from the garden;
homemade bread; playing in the irrigation water; racing with my
sisters to see who could shell the most peas; and early morning
raspberry picking "parties", as my sisters and I sarcastically

called them. Our family was typical of many of the neighbors, except that on our two-thirds of an acre we raised a variety of animals—chickens, ducks, geese, and even a lamb; and we grew not one, but two large gardens which produced an ample supply of vegetables to weed, harvest, and preserve.

My mother, who grew up on a dairy farm in upstate New York, understood the value of hard work; and we children became the unwilling beneficiaries of her unceasing ambition. We preserved everything Mom could get her hands on: peaches, pears, cherries, apricots, apples, berries, corn, peas, beans, beets, tomatoes, and spinach. I have vivid recollections of long summer days shelling bucket after bucket of peas and snapping the ends off of piles and piles of beans. When the beans in our garden ran out, Mom picked the neighbors' surplus. Sometimes I wondered if she did it just to torture us! Although the days were long and hot and the work was often tedious and messy and performed begrudgingly, the experience of working side by side with my siblings has created cherished memories and built friendships that continue to this day.

My husband, too, lived on a small farm in a rural community during his early childhood and has fond memories of helping to care for rabbits, chickens, pigs, a horse, and a cow. He also helped irrigate, weed the garden, and pick fruit. Although he was still quite young when he lived on the farm, his yearning for that lifestyle has never left him.

As a result of our upbringings, my husband and I felt a strong desire to continue these agricultural traditions with our own children. Our first home was on one-third acre, nearly half of which was in garden. We also had fruit trees, raspberries, dairy goats, chickens, an occasional turkey, and a dog. The children helped plant, water, weed, harvest, and preserve the vegetables in our garden; and we bought a variety of fruits and berries which were either canned or dried or made into juice, jam, jelly, or syrup. In addition to canning, the children were expected to help with the yard work—planting flowers, weeding, trimming, edging, and mowing. At age eight they were taught to milk the goats and were included in the rotation for milking, gathering eggs, and feeding and watering the animals. When the outside chores were finished, they helped with a variety of tasks inside as well—cooking, cleaning, ironing, dusting, washing dishes, and babysitting.

In today's world of pampered children, indulgences, allowances, and self-gratification, it almost sounds like child abuse. However, we later moved from that little house on a third acre; and it was interesting to listen to the children reminisce fondly about what they missed most: the garden, fresh corn-on-the-cob, home-canned peaches, baby chicks, and especially the goats. In fact, one son insists that he'll have goats when he grows up. As hard as the work was and as much as they may have complained at the time, something happened between the weeding and the watering, the milking and the mowing, and the cooking and the cleaning. More than a garden was grown, more than animals were tended, and more than meals were made. In the midst of working, they learned to love those they served and with whom they served, even the animals. Lifelong friendships were formed, memories were made, and emotional bridges were built that connect parents to children and sibling to sibling.

Of course, farming is not the only way to teach children to work. Opportunities for work are as varied as the individual. A brick mason can teach children the skills of his trade, likewise, a plumber, an electrician, a jeweler, a grocer, a seamstress, a chef, a woodcarver, or a fisherman. It is not so much about the type of work children do as it is about having a work experience. Working with and for others provides an enduring connectedness that will span the years.

Today's modern conveniences which are supposedly meant to improve the quality of our lives may not be all that they first appear. Food processors, dishwashers, and snowblowers may have eliminated the need for many people to be working at once; but they have also eliminated the opportunity to work together, learning to understand and get along with others. Certainly, we wouldn't want to return to the lifestyle of our grandparents; but we would do well to analyze the necessity of our modern conveniences, recognizing what we are giving up for the advantages we may gain.

Our family does not use a dishwasher. When the children complain, we simply say, "Why do we need another one, we have six already!" Unfortunately, they fail to see the humor in this as well as failing to see the advantages of standing side by side at the kitchen sink telling stories, singing songs, reciting scenes from a movie, and, yes, even arguing. Although they may not realize it now, their relationships with one another are being strengthened; and someday, hopefully, they will recall these dishwashing days with fondness.

Working together has been a way of life since families began. In agrarian societies, a family's very existence is dependent upon the efforts of all its members. At very young ages children assume adult responsibilities: chopping wood, clearing fields, hauling water, milking cows, feeding chickens, digging ditches, fixing meals, tending babies, and sewing clothes. No one questions the necessity of the work—children or parents. It is their way of life. And, contrary to the popular sentiment of our day, it doesn't hurt them. What it does do, however, is turn them into responsible adults with grit and character who understand the value of work and self-reliance.

In time, difficulty and challenges make men out of boys. It makes adults out of children. It creates depth of character and gives substance and meaning to our lives. Many of society's most respected leaders have come from difficult circumstances. They have known hardship and poverty and faced overwhelming odds; but have you ever heard them complain about their early morning paper routes, hauling hay, milking cows, or performing menial labor in order to make a few dollars to support their widowed mothers? On the contrary! These are the very things they tout as the stepping stones to the heights of greatness they have achieved.

Not long ago I was with a group of women who were discussing this very topic. An older woman in the group mentioned that when her children were small they did their chores without being asked. They just knew what was expected and did it. There were a few "oohs" and "ahhs", and I even heard someone remark, "Well, they don't do that today."

What an unfortunate commentary on our society. What has happened to our parenting in recent years? Have we become too soft? Do we give in too easily? Do we make too many excuses for our children? Are we turning out selfish, lazy, ungrateful children who think the world owes them a living? Perhaps, in the spirit of good parenting, we think our children need to be pampered and protected. I believe today's children—yours and mine—can still be taught the value of work. It's all a matter of establishing realistic expectations, providing adequate training, and holding them accountable for the stewardships we assign them.

Whether we live on thirty acres or the thirtieth floor of a high rise apartment building, opportunities can be found to teach our children to work. The size of our lot and our home are irrelative when it comes to teaching children to do a job well and to see it through to completion. These are skills that will bless our children's lives forever. They are skills that are greatly lacking in the work force today. Capability, dependability, and responsibility are some of the greatest gifts we can give our children.

Hard work, especially family work—the very work we do in our homes on a daily basis—can do much to change our children, our families and, in fact, our entire nation.

> Home is the center from which we define and understand the nature of everything we encounter in the world. The home . . . is not one thing among many in a world of things; nor is it merely the product of a culture. Rather, the world of things derives its sense, and a culture its significance, from their relationship to the home. Without the home, everything else in the world or in a culture is meaningless . . . By changing how we do family work, we can build character, link families, unite communities, and change nations. Helping one another nurture children, care for the land, prepare food, and clean homes can bind lives together. This is the power of the home economy, and it is the power, available in every home no matter how troubled, that can end the turmoil of the family and begin to change the world.[1]

We must not underestimate the healing power of working with and serving one another. It is therapy for the soul. As someone has keenly observed, "The heart is the happiest when it beats for others."

---

1. "World Congress of Families II," Kathleen Slaugh Bahr, Geneva, Nov. 14-17, 1999, pp. 3, 9 (http://www.worldcongress.org/gen99, speakers/gen99 bahr.htm).

1

CHANGING YOUR MINDSET

*Opportunity is missed by most of us because
it is dressed in coveralls and looks like
work.—Thomas Edison*

Some Typical Situations

Brenda's day begins early. At 5:00 a.m. she sets out breakfast and throws in a load of laundry. Then she prepares for work while braiding hair, dressing children, signing papers, and counting lunch money. Sighing heavily, she drops the children off at school on her way to work. After work, she does more laundry, shuttles children to soccer practice and piano lessons, listens to her first-grader read, practices spelling words with her third-grader, fixes dinner, irons a shirt, sweeps the floor, vacuums the living room, and makes a batch of cookies for the PTA bake sale. Then she falls into bed exhausted at 11:00 p.m. Overworked and overwhelmed, she feels resentful of her husband and children.

Sharon is a stay-at-home mom with three preschoolers. Every day is the same endless chain of chores. With a cranky baby on her hip, she runs here and there in a frenzied state—wiping noses, changing diapers, washing and folding laundry, cleaning and mopping, vacuuming and dusting, cooking meals and washing dishes; but at the end of the day, nothing seems to look any better than it did before she started. All she has to show for her work is dirty clothes, tousled hair, and makeup long since vanished (if she had any on in the first place). The children's noses are still runny and dirty laundry is already piling up, there are footprints across the kitchen floor, cracker crumbs on the carpet, and dirty dishes in the sink. Feeling discouraged and unappreciated, she wonders, "Why bother?"

Tom and Tonya left their children alone for just a few hours while they ran some errands. Upon their return, they found that a major hurricane had just hit their place, leaving a trail of damage in its wake. The kitchen was cluttered with dirty dishes and bits of food from their children's unrestrained, relentless prowling for sustenance. Toys were strewn about the house in chaotic fashion while the little ones ran dirty, half naked and unattended. No homework had been done; and the older children were lying about the house engrossed in television and Nintendo, oblivious to the destruction going on around them.

Sound familiar? If so, this book is for you!

"Housework Makes You Ugly"

Years ago, my mother-in-law gave me a little wooden, starry-eyed doll with kinky hair that pokes out in all directions. The caption on the front reads, "Housework makes you ugly." For a long time it sat on my kitchen counter—a cruel reminder of the reality of my situation.

My husband didn't like it. He thought it sent the wrong message to the children. I must confess, I secretly delighted in it. It validated my feelings of anger and frustration. I found silent sympathy in it when I felt tired and grumpy.

It's not that I mind housework so much, I just find it aggravating and annoying to clean the same thing five times in one day. I get tired of being a human street sweeper, running around tidying up after the children. And, even worse, I get tired of them coming along right behind me destroying everything I have just tidied up!

Recently, I read a newspaper article describing the incredible pressures women today feel regarding housework. The article suggested hiring a housekeeper. While this is certainly one solution, for many mothers it is cost prohibitive. Furthermore, it deprives our children of valuable opportunities for work and service. I would like to suggest that part of the solution to our housecleaning woes lies in better training of our children so they can help with more of the work. By so doing, there will be more time for organizing and managing the household, catching up on all those unfinished projects, or perhaps even pursuing some long-neglected personal interests.

My goal in writing this book is to help you learn what I have learned about delegation over the past thirteen years. Additionally, it is my goal that you learn to delegate without making many of the mistakes I have made. Hopefully, you will discover "a more beautiful you" as the work is accomplished more efficiently; and you are left feeling less tired, less grumpy, and, consequently, less ugly.

Poor Management Syndrome

Before going any further, let's take a quick survey[1] to see if you suffer from Poor Management Syndrome (PMS). Answer yes or no to each of the following statements:

1. I don't have time to teach my children to work.

2. I feel like I need to nag in order for anything to get done.

3. My children have assigned chores, but they don't do them.

4. I do a lot of housework after the children go to bed.

5. When I am gone for any period of time, the house turns into a disaster area.

---

1. *Delegate,* Harold L. Taylor, Warner Books, New York, NY, 1989, 25-28. (Wording changed to fit a home situation rather than the office.)

6. When my children do work, it is often sloppily done.

7. I am so busy cleaning house that I don't have time for hobbies, skills, or talents.

8. I have physical ailments caused by too much stress.

9. My children are frequently bored or spend too much time watching television or playing computer games.

10. My children usually complain when asked to help with chores.

11. I am too controlling; I want everything done my way.

12. I'm always so tired and grouchy by the end of the day; I don't feel like doing anything with my spouse or family.

Did you find yourself saying, "Yes, yes, yes?" If so, this book is definitely for you.

I Was Reluctant to Delegate in the Beginning

Quite by accident, I learned the value of getting children to help around the house. It started many years ago, shortly after the birth of my fourth child. I had a new baby and a two-, four-, and six-year-old. I was homeschooling my six-year-old and my four-year-old was begging to learn to read. To top it all off, my husband was working full-time while finishing up his dissertation for a doctoral degree in the evenings. In short, life was overwhelming! (Today, with ten children, I look back on that time as the good ol' days. Nonetheless, it was all I could handle at the time.)

One evening after a tearful account of the day's events, my husband felt compelled to offer some advice. (All I really wanted was a listening ear and a little sympathy!) After a quick computation of all available data, he came up with the simplest, most obvious, logical answer, and said frankly, as only a man can say, "You need to get the children helping more."

"Oh, sure!" I complained. "What can a two-, four-, and six-year-old do?"

He suggested several tasks: mopping floors, cleaning the bathroom, folding laundry, dumping garbage.

I winced. "Not my babies! They're too little for such manual labor. I'm the mother; it's my job to take care of them. Besides, they wouldn't do a very good job anyway; and it would be more hassle than it was worth."

But my husband persisted. We had a lengthy discussion—my husband suggesting tasks that I felt were above my children's abilities, me countering with excuses why they couldn't do them. I must admit, I was rather skeptical; but then I really didn't have a choice. I could either continue doing what I was doing, which was obviously not working, or I could try his way. At length we reached a compromise on the tasks the children would be assigned, and I reluctantly agreed to give it a try. (I figured a few weeks would be sufficient time to prove it wouldn't work, and then he wouldn't bother me about it anymore!)

A few days later, we held a family council to "drop the bomb". Little did our children know that their simple, carefree lives were about to change forever. First, my husband enumerated all the responsibilities Mom and Dad had and how hard it was to get everything done. Then, he made the proposal that the children would assume some of these tasks, to ease the burden somewhat.

After listening intently, six-year-old Trenton asked inquisitively, "How long do we have to do this?"

"Forever," my husband replied matter-of-factly.

There was considerable silence while Trenton mulled this over and then solemnly declared, "I would be glad to help . . . but not forever." We quickly did some back pedaling, trying to soften the blow; and the two oldest at last agreed to help.

This is a list of the chores that were delegated to the children at that time. Although they had already been doing many of these tasks on a sporadic, informal basis, they now became *permanently delegated* tasks:

mopping floors	setting and clearing the table
cleaning up toys	vacuuming
helping with canning	making their beds
emptying the garbage	fixing simple meals
cleaning the bathroom	folding underwear and
folding diapers	matching socks
dusting	

It seems like quite a bit for a four- and six-year-old, but I was amazed at how well they did. I was also amazed at the difference it made for me. There *was* a way; there *was* hope; these little children could make a difference. (As difficult as it is to admit, *his* way worked!)

Since that first family council, our family has grown considerably and so have the children's responsibilities. We eventually bought a small home with a large lot on which we planted a substantial garden. Naturally, the list of delegated tasks became longer. Today, we have a larger home on three and a half acres; and, again, the children's responsibilities have grown. Today their chores include:

helping with laundry	pulling weeds in
picking vegetables	garden/flower beds
shelling peas/drying fruit	mowing the lawn
ironing	fixing meals
washing dishes	changing sheets on beds
gathering eggs	dressing and bathing
feeding/watering the animals	younger children
shoveling snow	raking leaves
watering the garden	irrigating the pasture
	changing oil in vehicles

At first glance, it seems like a lot. But, remember, they don't do all these things every day, nor do they do all of these things year round. And, again, I am impressed with how well they have done and at the difference it makes for me.

Children Are Assets, Not Liabilities

Effective delegation occurs when we begin to think of our children as assets rather than liabilities. Perhaps, like me, you sometimes find yourself starting a countdown for bedtime right after dinner (or perhaps before)! Or, maybe you can't wait for the children to start back to school at the end of a long summer vacation. Instead of viewing the time our children are home as a hectic, miserable experience merely to be endured, we can make use of this valuable time by having tasks and projects for them to do. Not only will the time pass more quickly for everyone, but it will be much more pleasant. By tapping into our children's vast reserves of time and energy, we can fill their spare time with worthwhile activities while simultaneously teaching them the value of work and completing many of our own overdue projects.

Summer is a great time to get some concentrated help from your children. One summer my children and I all worked together refinishing three antique wooden chairs that had been in our shed for years. My husband had threatened to throw them out several times, but I kept insisting that I was going to refinish them. I decided this would be the summer—before it was too late.

Every morning, right after chores were completed, and before everyone started their individual projects, we sanded on the chairs for 30-45 minutes. It took six of us two months of serious sanding to complete the project, and for a while it looked as though we had taken on an impossible task. I must confess, if I were doing it alone, I probably would have given up; but since the children had already invested so much time, I felt obliged to finish. Nevertheless, when the chairs were at last stained and varnished, complete with new cloth seat coverings, we all felt the satisfaction that comes from knowing we had accomplished something difficult yet wonderful. It was a powerful bonding experience for all of us.

You are the Conductor of Your Own Home Orchestra

For a moment, imagine yourself as the conductor of a great orchestra. It is opening night; as the curtain parts, the audience is stunned to see a solitary figure standing on the stage. First, you play a few notes on the violin, then you run to play the trumpet, then the tuba, then dash back to play the violin again. Not only would it take an incredibly long time to get through a piece of music, but the resulting sound would be choppy and disjointed and, in fact, most unpleasant. Certainly, no one would argue the merits of individual musicians each playing a single instrument which, when blended simultaneously with the entire orchestra, produce a symphony of beauty and harmony.

Likewise, housework is not a one man or woman show. As the parent, you are not a soloist but rather the conductor of your own home orchestra. You need not, in fact, you *should not* try to do all the work yourself. There is no need to run haphazardly from task to task trying to make melody out of discord and chaos. Like the musicians in an orchestra, each member of the family should have specific, individual assignments; thus, establishing a symphony of siblings. As the conductor, your job is to supervise and coordinate, indeed, to orchestrate the various assignments in the formation of a family masterpiece in which all the work is accomplished in an efficient, timely fashion, everyone working together harmoniously (at least once in a while). To set the stage, so to speak, let me begin with an example of what can happen with effective delegation.

A Personal Experience

One Saturday, I had gone to an early morning meeting, leaving the house around 7:00 a.m. When I returned at 9:30 a.m., my husband and seven children had already dressed, eaten breakfast, washed the dishes, cleaned the kitchen, made their beds, scrubbed the bathrooms, vacuumed the floors, and my eleven-year-old son was just finishing with the mopping in the kitchen. The house felt peaceful and refreshing, and I sank into a comfortable chair to enjoy a few moments of silence as I unwound from a busy morning.

Before you jump to any conclusions, let me assure you it is not like this every Saturday. If the truth were known, some Saturday mornings we are just finishing breakfast at 9:30 and still trying to get started on the day. This particular morning, my husband was exceptionally ambitious; and I was pleasantly surprised *and* most grateful.

The point of this story is to help you realize that as a parent, you don't have to do it all. Children *can* work without you there, and the house doesn't need to fall apart just because you are gone.

Fathers Are Invaluable

While much of what is said in this book is directed to mothers, who typically bear the greater burden for running the household, it applies equally to fathers. Their support and cooperation is crucial. Mom and Dad should provide a united front in the formidable task of teaching children to work. The more father is involved, the more effective delegation becomes. I appreciate it when my husband assumes the responsibility for getting the children working. It temporarily relieves me of the burden and is a welcome break. Besides, it's no fun being the only tough guy in the family. Delegation works best when there are no disagreements between parents on what will be done, how it will be done, or who will do it.

Fathers tend to be better delegators. Whenever my husband oversees a task—inside or out, I can generally be sure he'll get several of the children helping. Delegation seems to come more naturally to men. (I wonder if it is desperation or a deliberate attempt to diminish the delinquency of their children.) Whatever the case, you would do well to capitalize on this innate character trait.

My husband, Bruce, enjoys doing Dutch oven cooking. It is his hobby, so to speak. What this really means is that he prepares the pots while the children are busy in the kitchen: chopping, stirring, cutting, and grating. Bruce spends most of the time giving orders, tapping the briquettes to keep them burning, and poking the food with toothpicks to see if it is done. It has become a family joke that whenever Dad decides to do Dutch oven, most, if not all, of the family will be involved in some way. We enjoy giving him a hard time about it, and he takes it good naturedly. But, whenever he tells someone that he does Dutch oven cooking, the rest of us just smile, casting sideways glances at each other. After all, we know the truth!

But, then, that's exactly what delegation is all about—accomplishing great things through others. And we don't really mind because, in the end, we all benefit from a delicious Dutch oven dinner. I have to admit, he does come up with some good ones— barbecued ribs, lemon chicken, cheesy potatoes, and the best berry pie you have ever tasted! He always says, "Everything tastes better when it's cooked in a Dutch oven."

Fathers can be great role models. The mere presence of father alters the mood in the home; and children tend to work better when he is around, especially if he sets the example. This is extremely important for sons. In addition to the traditional male tasks, let them see Dad cooking, sweeping, vacuuming, bathing children, and changing diapers. Father can have a profound influence on his children's attitude towards work. You will have better results if this most important task is a shared responsibility between both parents.

Many Hands Make Light Work

That's what delegation is all about. It's about working together for common goals—everyone sharing the work and doing their part. It's about teaching children to work, to take pride in what they do, and to be accountable for the tasks that are theirs, thereby experiencing the feeling of achievement and consequent self-respect that come from fulfilling their responsibility. When everyone in the family does a little, the family can accomplish great things.

I Am Not An Expert

Before going any further, I need to give a brief disclaimer. You need to know that I do not have a degree in child psychology, home management or delegation nor have I had any professional training on the subject. My only training has been "on-the-job" in the ongoing struggle to raise ten children. In no way do I profess to be an expert, *unless* an expert can be defined as someone who has learned something through a lot of trial and error and a lot of tears and frustration. Under this definition, I most definitely qualify!

Most of what I have learned and what I will share with you, has come from the road of hard knocks and from a deeply held personal conviction of the power of work and the merits of a good day's labor. Over the years I have refined and added to this process of delegation, and I have learned a few tips which I will share with you. I hope you find them insightful and useful.

2

DELEGATION: YOUR KEY TO SANITY

*The only place where success comes before
work is a dictionary.—Vidal Sassoon*

Camouflaged Slave Labor?

My husband facetiously defines delegation as camouflaged
slave labor; and sometimes, I must admit, our children think
that's exactly what it is! When I mentioned this to my oldest
daughter one day, she exclaimed, "Mom, there's nothing camouflaged about it!"

However, a more scholarly definition can be found in Harold
Taylor's book, *Delegate—The Key to Successful Management:*

> Leadership is not the process of accomplishing great things
> by ourselves. . . . It is rather the process of accomplishing great
> things through our [children], thereby raising their self-
> respect. Leadership also involves more than simply overseeing
> or directing others. It involves developing [children's] skills
> through delegation. [Delegation] . . . does not mean dumping
> work onto someone without prior training. . . or constantly
> delegating to the same [child]. Nor does it mean always
> assigning all the boring, meaningless tasks. Delegation devel-
> ops people who are able to work independently with a mini-
> mum of direction.[1]

---

1. *Delegate,* Harold L. Taylor, Warner Books, Inc., New York, NY,
1989, pp. 15, 16, 22.

Family counselor James Dobson puts it quite succinctly, "Our objective as parents . . . is to do nothing for boys and girls which they can profit from doing themselves." And, Paul Lewis has said, "Remember, your basic job as a parent is to work yourself out of a job." The true test of successful delegation is how well your children work alone or when you are gone.

Permanent Delegation

Basically, there are two types of delegation: *permanent* and *spontaneous.* Permanent delegation, as the name suggests, is assigned tasks that children know they need to perform daily, weekly, monthly, or seasonally. Thursday night may be their night to do dishes, or they may need to feed the dog every morning before going to school, or perhaps it is their job to shovel the driveway each time it snows. They know it is expected of them and they can plan for it.

When my two little ones first started folding underwear and matching socks, it was a monumental task, sometimes taking two hours to complete because they dawdled so much. When I did laundry, they knew they would be expected to match socks; and so it was with great anxiety that they would ask, "Is today sock day?"

My children also know they will be expected to clean up their toys when they are finished playing. One day, five-year-old Jarom wanted to play with the Daktari jungle set. This ends up making quite a mess with trees and cages and jungle animals scattered across the floor. Nevertheless, as I carried the box to the living room, he informed me that he would clean it up because "that was just part of life."

At our home, we have a daily, rotating schedule for washing dishes, rinsing dishes, sweeping the floor, cleaning the bathroom sink, and helping with dinner. Our more thorough housecleaning is done on Saturday, and we have a rotating schedule for these chores, too. The children know they will be held accountable for the completion of their work; and sometimes, on their own initiative, they will do their chores Friday afternoon if they have commitments Saturday morning.

The specifics of what will be done and who will do it were decided in a family council where everyone had a chance to give input. The secret to successful permanent delegation is accountability and appropriate consequences when assigned tasks are not completed which is discussed further in the *Six D's of Delegation.*

Spontaneous Delegation

The second kind of delegation is spontaneous delegation. This means tasks or assignments that are delegated due to extenuating circumstances such as emergencies, illness, or unexpected company. At this time, for example, I call the children together and explain that Dad has invited someone to dinner and I need some help preparing food and tidying up the house. Each child is then assigned one or more tasks; and somehow we manage to clean the house, set the table, and prepare the food with a delicious aroma filling the air as my husband, all smiles, saunters in the house ten minutes before the guests arrive!

I remember one spontaneous incident vividly. It was my oldest son's fifteenth birthday. Just as I walked into the kitchen to begin preparing his special birthday dinner, my eleven-year-old son entered from the opposite direction, carefully cradling his right arm with a look of pain and panic on his face. One look at the unusually large lump protruding from his wrist told me that it was broken. My mind immediately began spinning—what to do with the broken arm (this was a new experience for us), should I call my husband, should I call the doctor, and what about the birthday dinner—should we postpone it until another night? After making a few phone calls, I gathered the children together, explaining that Dad and I would be taking Caleb to the hospital. I then proceeded to give instructions to each of the children. One would be in charge of cooking the noodles, another the sauce, another the salad, and someone else would set the table, etc. After everything had been assigned, we left for the hospital.

When we returned home two hours later, I was surprised by what I found. Not only was dinner ready; but the table was set, complete with tablecloth and candles; the drapes were drawn; and soft, classical music was playing, creating a relaxing, peaceful mood which was a delightful treat after a hectic afternoon. I guess my son figured if he had to fix his own birthday dinner, he may as well make the best of it!

Mother Bunny Delegates

We have a classic children's book, *The Country Bunny and the Little Gold Shoes,* which illustrates perfectly what can happen with successful delegation. It is the story of a little girl bunny whose secret desire is to one day be chosen as the new Easter Bunny. However, she eventually marries and ends up with twenty-one baby bunnies. With all these babies to care for, it seems that her dream of being the Easter Bunny will never come true.

As the babies grow older, however, Mother Bunny realizes that her little bunnies are now capable of assuming responsibilities around the house, so she calls them all together to give them assignments. She teaches some of them to sweep, some to mend and sew, some to make beds, cook, wash dishes, do laundry, and work in the garden. With her children now doing much of the work, Mother Bunny once again has some free time.

When the Easter Bunny eventually dies, Mother Bunny decides to try for the job. The problem is that wise, old Grandfather Bunny doesn't think Mother Bunny could possibly take on this extra assignment because she needs to be home taking care of her many children. However, after Mother Bunny carefully explains how each of her children has a job to do around the house, allowing her time for other things, Grandfather Bunny at last agrees to let her be the new Easter Bunny.

On Easter Eve, after Mother Bunny has been out all night delivering goodies, she returns home to find ". . . that the garden was tended . . . . The floors were swept and there were two lovely new pictures painted and hanging on the wall. The dishes were washed and shone in the cupboard. The clothes were washed and mended and nicely hung away. And her twenty-one children were all sound asleep in their little beds."[2]

Now, just a minute; I know exactly what you're thinking, "Cute story, but it's just a fairy tale. It never happens that way in real life." But what if I told you it could happen that way. In fact, I can tell you from personal experience that it has happened that way in our home—more than once, by the way, which leads me to believe it wasn't an accident!

When my husband and I go out in the evenings, we return to find that dinner has been prepared, the dishes washed, the kitchen cleaned, the toys picked up, and the little ones diapered and put to bed if it is bedtime. Now that we have teenagers, the older children are not usually in bed when we get home; but when they were younger, all the children would be in bed sound asleep when we returned. What a wonderful feeling to know that things are taken care of while we are gone, and my husband and I often express to each other and to the children our appreciation for their dependability.

2. *The Country Bunny and the Little Gold Shoes,* DuBose Heyward, Houghton Mifflin Company, New York, NY, 1967.

Rules of Delegation

Amazing things can happen with delegation. I am still amazed at times, even after all these years. However, there are a few simple rules necessary for success. I will refer to these rules throughout the book, so it is important to understand them now. They are:

- **Be Firm, Be Fair, Be Flexible**
- **Be Patient**
- **Be Tolerant**
- **Be Specific**

Rule 1: Be Firm, Be Fair, Be Flexible

In other words, be consistent yet considerate. Make rules, set guidelines, and establish appropriate consequences for disobedience. At the same time, recognize that children have extenuating circumstances, too. Be willing to adjust.

Be firm. Don't give in to your children's fussing or complaining just because they're trying to get out of work, they're angry about doing the work, or they're eager to play or watch television. They need to understand that they have responsibilities around the house, and they will be expected to complete them (*Discipline*, 34-42).

Be fair. Be sensitive to the needs and abilities of your children. Set reasonable expectations. What is fair for one child, may not be fair for another. Tailor tasks to fit their unique capacities and circumstances. Thus, you can challenge them without overwhelming them.

While my fifteen-year-old is quite capable of vacuuming the entire house, I would not expect the same of my five-year-old, although he could certainly vacuum a room or two. Likewise, I might ask my eighteen-year-old to pick all the apples on the apple tree; but this same task would overwhelm my eight-year-old. A more realistic assignment for my eight-year-old would be to pick a bushel or two a day—a task he could accomplish because it had set parameters.

At our home, the children join the rotation of dishwashing, chores, and mowing the lawn when they turn eight. However, one son is rather small for his age; and at eight, he was definitely too small to mow the lawn. Therefore, we waited a year before assigning him this task. Even at nine, he struggled to mow his section of the lawn; and we often helped him with the chore.

Be flexible—allow for their emergencies. If a child has an important test or big school project due the next day and it's his night to do dishes, let him trade with another child. If a child is too sick to do her work, move on to the next person in the rotation or have everyone pitch in to cover for her. If someone has an activity that requires him to be gone all evening, don't holler to him as he walks out the door, "The dishes will be here when you get back." No one likes to come home at ten o'clock at night to a messy kitchen and a sink full of dirty dishes.

Last summer, my daughter took a microbiology class at the local university. Due to the intensity of the class, we didn't ask her to do very much yard work. Besides, the other children were out of school and had more free time; and it was not too burdensome on them to pick up some of the slack.

Be careful that your children don't take advantage of your kindness. There can be a temptation for children to be "sick" longer than necessary, to always have a lot of homework, or to drag one project out in order to avoid helping with a second project. Everyone has an occasional emergency; but, as the word implies, emergencies occur infrequently. Be careful that they don't become a habit.

Be firm. Be fair. Be flexible. You will find that if you are willing to work with your children, they will be more willing to work with you.

Rule 2: Be Patient

It will probably take your children longer than you expect to get the hang of it, especially your little ones. Little children are still mastering their hand-eye coordination, and those little hands—and even the not-so-little hands—can be so slow and awkward at times (except, of course, when they're getting into things they aren't supposed to). Seemingly simple projects can be major events for children.

If you ask your eight-year-old to cut tomatoes, for example, you need to allow sufficient time for completion of the project. First, he will need to sort through all the knives, carefully selecting the one most suited for the project. Perhaps he will even need to try several of them to determine which one works best. When he washes the tomatoes, he will probably be distracted by the running water, becoming enthralled as it cascades over the dirty utensils he has found lying in the sink. Or, as the sink fills with water, he may become so absorbed with the various floating objects that he completely forgets about the task at hand. You will find him sometime later, happily splashing about—not a care in the world!

Children are immune to many of the pressures we feel as adults. Time means nothing to my four-year-old. I was talking to him about an upcoming event one day, explaining that it would happen "tomorrow". Inquisitively, he asked, "What's tomorrow?" This little guy measures time and days by events: Sunday is church day, Tuesday is laundry day, and Saturday is when Dad and all the kids are home. At our house we have granola for breakfast on Sunday because it is quick and easy when preparing for church. On occasion when we have it on a day other than Sunday, this same little guy will look at me and innocently ask, "Is today church day?"

Deadlines, time constraints, and multi-tasking are foreign concepts to small children. Speed is simply not an issue. Be patient—as frustrating as it may be at times, in fact, much of the time. Delegation is a process, sometimes a long, slow process depending on the age and capacity of your children. If you can keep in mind that the goal is not speed but raising responsible, capable children, patience will come much easier.

Rule 3: Be Tolerant

Be willing to accept less than perfection. Closely linked to patience, is the third rule of delegation: tolerance. Again, keep in mind that the goal is to raise responsible children.

I remember well my own internal struggle when my four-year-old daughter first started mopping the bathroom floor. It was not as clean as I would have liked, and I agonized over my conflicting feelings. One side of me understood how important it was for her to do this job by herself, yet the other side of me wanted the job done well. At length, I opted to forego my own need for cleanliness, accepting her best effort for the sake of the greater good that would be achieved in the long term. With practice, her work gradually improved.

Occasionally, however, when I just couldn't live with it, I locked the bathroom door and redid parts of the floor, being careful that she never knew. If children find out you've redone their work, the negative results are two-fold: first, their self-esteem suffers; and, second, they learn that they really don't have to do a good job because Mom or Dad will just do it again anyway.

The quality of the work is not nearly as important as the lessons your children are learning. This is especially true with young children. Naturally, the older the child, the greater your expectation that the work will be done well.

At any given moment, there is bound to be clutter somewhere. Before I was married, I had visions of an immaculately clean home—tidy closets and drawers, spotless countertops, neatly made beds, and bathroom chrome that sparkled. Today, with ten children, I have learned to tolerate a certain degree of clutter. Unless I spend all day cleaning house, it simply isn't possible—or reasonable—to keep it completely clean all the time.

I once heard someone say that their home was clean enough to be healthy but dirty enough to be happy. There is much truth in that statement. Obviously, everyone has a different tolerance level for clutter; but don't be too harsh on your children.

Someday, when the children are grown, I will wash down all the walls and straighten all the drawers and closets. When I wander from room to room, there will be a place for everything and everything will be in its place. Imagine! How peaceful. How serene. . . . How eerie and quiet and lonely . . . but that day is not today. Today I am raising kids, and kids create clutter!

Rule 4: Be Specific

Never assume anything. Do not suppose it's clear to your child how to do a given chore. Being very specific at the outset about what you want done and how it should be done can prevent a lot of frustration for parent and child. Too often we take it for granted that our children will know how to do simple projects, only to find out later, much to our chagrin, that they really *didn't* know how to do it.

When asked if he would clean the bathtub, one young man asked if he should clean the outside, too. A bit surprised by the question, his mother answered, "Why, yes." When she came back a while later, she found him spraying the outside of the tub with the shower massage!

Camille cuts grapefruit. One morning I asked nine-year-old Camille to cut the grapefruit for breakfast. She replied confidently that she would, and so I assumed she knew how to do it. Without any instruction, I left her to the task. (After all, how difficult can it be to cut grapefruit? It didn't take long to find out!) She cut the very first grapefruit parallel to the grapefruit sections rather than perpendicular. Realizing my mistake, I showed her the correct way to do it, leaving her once again without any further instruction. She did quite well until the last grapefruit, which she cut unevenly, resulting in a very small piece and a very large piece. By this time I was rather annoyed, and it showed. I had asked her to do this simple task to relieve some of my stress, but instead she had created more. "I should have done it myself," I thought. She sensed my irritation and felt dejected. A few moments of simple explanation could have avoided this whole problem.

Isaac tapes the bag of laundry soap. Another time, I opened a twenty-pound bag of laundry soap to refill the bucket that I keep in the laundry room. I used about one-third of the bag and asked Isaac to roll down the top of the bag, "tape it up", and take it back downstairs. He seemed happy to help and went off without any questions. I didn't think any more about it until a few days later when I went to the fruit room to get something. There was the bag of soap, well secured with about ten strips of duct tape! "Ugggh," I thought. "What has he done? That is way too much tape and duct tape is so expensive!" This thought was immediately followed with, "Well, it's your own fault. You really didn't give any specific directions."

When I asked my son to "tape the bag", I had a mental picture of what I expected—one little piece of tape in the center of the bag, just enough to keep it rolled down; but I had failed to convey any of this to him. He really wasn't trying to be difficult—it's just that his vision of "taping" was different from mine. A few simple instructions could have ensured that we both shared the same vision.

How Do I Begin?

The Six D's of Delegation

Now that you understand the basic rules of delegation, you're ready to tackle the big question that has probably been nagging at the back of your mind all along, "How do I start?" This can be summed up in what I call the Six D's of Delegation. By following these basic steps, you can tailor a system of delegation unique to the needs of your particular family:

- **Decide:** what jobs can be delegated
- **Divide:** the jobs among family members
- **Deliberate:** any inequalities or challenges and redistribute tasks if necessary
- **Demonstrate:** the *what, why,* and *how*—provide adequate training
- **Discipline:** accountability, consequences, and consistency
- **Determination:** you can do it!

The First "D": Decide What Jobs Can Be Delegated

Deciding what jobs can be delegated is the first step of delegation and, perhaps, one of the more difficult. This is the time for personal introspection as you ask yourself some hard questions:

- Why is delegation even important or necessary?
- What do I hope to accomplish with delegation?
- What are my personal and emotional needs?
- What jobs am I willing to delegate to my children?
- How much are they capable of doing?

There will be a real temptation to make excuses for your children or to feel guilty about passing on some of "your" work to your children. It is only natural. We all want to be the nice guy, but this is the time to be serious and realistic about what *you* can do and what *your children* can do. Besides, it really isn't "your" work; it's the family's work. Your children dirty the bathroom and eat off the dishes, so it's only fair that they help clean up. For your own sake and for the sake of your children, resist the urge to be too lenient. Remember, delegation is not just about the benefits of passing on some of your work; it is about finding work for your children, thereby keeping them busy and out of trouble, raising their self-esteem, and teaching them responsibility.

After you have done some serious soul searching, sit down with your spouse, if you are married, and discuss your plan. Maybe he can help you brainstorm. He may make suggestions you haven't considered. Even if your spouse doesn't have much to add, it is critical that he is aware of the plan *before* you present it to the children and that the two of you are in complete agreement—or have at least reached an acceptable compromise.

When the two of you have ironed out all the wrinkles, you are then ready to present your plan to the children. This should be done in an official family council, thereby creating the impression that this is something important and that you are serious about what you will be discussing. (Family councils are discussed in greater detail under *Deliberate*, 27-30.)

The Second "D": Divide the Jobs Among Family Members

I have already mentioned how the division of chores was done initially in our family when the children were still very small. It was a decision my husband and I made and then told the children what they needed to do. This worked fine when they were small, but I can guarantee this approach will not work well with older children—especially teenagers.

Everyone should have a voice in the division of chores. With older children, we now sit together and discuss various options as a family, eventually reaching an agreement on what will be done. Sometimes we reach this conclusion by general consensus; other times we end up voting on it. It is important to note that while we try to please everyone, everyone may not be completely happy every time.

You may not always get the division of chores just right the first time. When our three younger boys first started dumping garbage, it was always a fight. First, they complained because they didn't want to do it. Then when they did do it, they fought over which garbage cans they would dump and who had dumped more than another. I got tired of the hassle.

Finally, I decided to try a different approach. I assigned each of the boys specific garbage cans they were responsible for dumping. It worked great! There was no more fighting over who had done more than another or who should do which garbage. It was a simple change, but it made a big difference.

Years ago, when the older children first started doing dishes, everyone helped clear the table, then two of the children washed and rinsed the dishes. Clearing the table took forever. For some reason, it seemed to be an agonizing chore. My guess is that the washer and rinser weren't excited about clearing the table *and* doing the dishes, so they tried to clear as little as possible. Because they were working so slowly, everyone else did, too. Everyone was subtly trying to do as little as possible.

For a long time, I wondered what could be done to make things go more quickly. Finally, I decided that if the washer did not clear the table, they could get started immediately on the dishes. This helped somewhat, but then we had the problem of dishes piling up in the rinser's sink because they were still busy clearing the table. It became obvious that the rinser should also be excused from clearing in order to get right to the dishes.

Things got a little better with this approach, but we still had trouble getting the table cleared. The dishwasher often finished washing everything on the counters and had to wait for the table to be cleared.

At last I came up with what has turned out to be—if I do say so myself—a clever solution. If the table is not cleared by the time the dishwasher gets everything washed on the counter, the clearers must wash the remaining dishes. It has worked marvelously!

There have been a few times the washer has "got them", as we call it. But the greater problem now, if you can call it a problem, is that the clearers are too efficient. Sometimes they start cleaning up before I am even finished with my meal. Between cutting meat, buttering toast, checking food in the oven, and caring for the baby, it takes me longer to eat than the rest of the family; and there have been times when my plate has been swiped away from me with food still on it!

The division of chores is constantly changing. This is where you practice flexibility. It is also where family councils, as discussed in the next section, become so important.

During the summer, we have a dishwashing rotation that changes each meal: one child washes, one rinses, and one sweeps the kitchen floor. When school starts again, however, the dishwashing schedule also changes since all of the older children are now gone in the morning. So, we make other adjustments. This year, Isaac and Jarom do breakfast dishes as well as the outside chores, while Camille and Abram do lunch dishes. The four oldest children continue the regular rotation for the evening meal and on the weekends, except that Isaac also joins the rotation on the weekend.

I know it sounds complicated, but the children know exactly how it works. They should; after all, they helped make the rules. There are so many exceptions and inclusions due to their insistence on fairness. Of course, no one wants to do more than their share; and this is what we have worked out to make it seem fair to everyone. This works for now; but when school is out again, we'll have to think of something different. And, we'll have to make changes again in a year or so when Abram turns eight and joins the rotation.

Delegation is constantly changing and evolving. Just when you think you've got a system that works, something is bound to change. Accept it, work it out, and move on. Remember, flexibility is the first rule of delegation.

The Third "D": Deliberate—Hold Regular Family Councils

Family councils are similar to board meetings. They are the coming together of ideas, complaints, and concerns. This is the time and place to work out disagreements and find solutions to your problems in an environment of cooperation. That is not to say that some of these "discussions" don't get rather loud and lively, but everyone must be allowed to express their point of view without fear of ridicule or sarcasm from other family members. They must feel their contribution is important and that their vote counts. There will be some give and take by everyone, but you should eventually be able to reach a compromise that is satisfactory to all.

If my husband or I feel strongly about a certain issue or about how something should be done, we can steer the conversation in that direction. And sometimes we may detect hurt or anger in one or more of the children and will work to alleviate those feelings. We have also found that we may need to help them come to closure as there is a tendency to rehash the same things over and over. However, as long as the debate isn't out of control, we let the children work out many of the details of what and how things will be done themselves. After all, they are the direct beneficiaries of the discussion.

A family council in action. When we moved back from Hawaii, we needed to decide how the chores would be divided in our new home since it was larger and had a much different floor plan. So, we sat together as a family, discussing possible ways to divide the chores. There was considerable discussion and many possibilities presented before we finally arrived at a satisfactory solution. This is what we came up with:

Person 1—mopping kitchen and entry way, dusting, mowing part of lawn

Person 2—vacuuming entire house, mowing lawn

Person 3—cleaning master bath, mowing lawn

Person 4—cleaning laundry room and bath, sweeping back porch, mowing lawn

Person 5—cleaning main bath, sweeping front porch, mowing lawn

Jarom, Abram, Levi—dumping garbage

A few months later, we cut out the carpet under the kitchen table, replacing it with linoleum. (Carpet under the kitchen table just doesn't work with small children.) Since this greatly increased the amount of kitchen mopping to be done, we again met as a family and discussed what to do. It was decided that the entry way would now be mopped by the person who cleaned and mopped the laundry room.

Then, a few months later, when our son, Jarom, turned eight, we had another family council. We have found that eight is a good age to move children out of the smaller jobs and blend with the older children in the dishwashing and housecleaning rotations. And now that Jarom had reached this magical age, we needed to discuss what he would do and how the chores would be redistributed to include him.

After much debate, it was finally decided to keep things simple for him at this time. He would take on the task of mopping the entry way and sweeping the back porch every week in addition to his regular job of dumping garbage. However, since he was doing more work on Saturday, his two younger brothers would dump his garbage on that day. We also decided that Abram, now almost seven, could take on the added responsibility of sweeping the front porch.

Gradually increase responsibilities. We have found it easier to get children working if you gradually increase their responsibilities. Abram has been making his bed and dumping garbage for years. He also helps set and clear the table, clean up toys, and pull weeds. He is now assuming the added responsibility of sweeping the front porch and helping with lunch dishes. When he turns eight, we will add even more. This way we can ease him into the work cycle without overwhelming him.

Recently, we have added another dimension to our family councils. With three teenagers and a twelve-year-old who thinks she's a teenager, we have found that we need to have a weekly planning meeting to discuss their various activities. On Sunday evening, we gather with the calendar to write down the events of the week. Not only does this help with scheduling, but it also helps see potential conflicts with chores and how they can be resolved. Someone may need to switch nights for doing dishes, or, due to some family activity, Saturday chores may need to be done on a day other than Saturday. If the children know this ahead of time, there will less complaining and fussing later in the week when you remind them of the change.

That's the beauty of family councils: to analyze what is and is not working and to come up with satisfactory solutions. In the end, everyone is clear about what the new plan is and how it works. And, hopefully, everyone is happy with it. We always try to end on a positive note. Do not underestimate the ability and

willingness of your children to help work through the problems.
They can come up with some rather insightful solutions. After
all, they have a vested interest in the final decision.

The Fourth "D": Demonstrate—Provide Adequate Training

Adequate training is essential to successful delegation. Without it, you end up with a lot of sloppy work and a lot of frustration. This takes time, sometimes a lot of time if your children are
still small, but the investment is certainly worth it. A few hours
of careful training now will reap large dividends for you in the
days ahead.

**There are three important areas to cover when training
your children on new tasks: what, why, and how.** Don't just
tell your children *what* to do; you must also tell them *why* they
need to do what they're doing and show them *how*—even when
they say they already know. Go through the entire process, step
by step, discussing and asking questions as you go. By asking
questions rather than merely showing or telling them what to do,
you encourage critical thinking and active listening; and the
child will better understand *why* you're doing *what* you're doing.

At our house, we mop floors with a bucket of water and a rag
so we can better clean the edges and the corners. Several years
ago when Jadee first started mopping the kitchen floor, I noticed
the floor was taking much too long to dry—sometimes more
than an hour—and it was aggravating when I couldn't get into
the kitchen to do my work. After a couple of weeks, I finally told
her to wring the rag out better so the floor wasn't so wet. Then I
began to notice that the floor didn't seem to be getting as clean
as it should, so I decided to watch her mop. First, she squeezed
the rag so completely dry there was hardly any water left, then
with it still wadded in a little ball, she proceeded to mop. The
problem became obvious immediately—not only was the rag too

dry to really clean, but with it all rolled up, she was missing parts of the floor as she wiped back and forth. Clearly, the dirty floor was a reflection of poor training; and right then we had a lesson on the proper way to mop the floor.

Dipping the rag in the bucket, I pulled it out dripping wet. "What's wrong with this?" I asked. (Notice the use of questions which helps the child think through the process. They'll remember longer and understand better if they have thought it through themselves.) Then I wrung the rag so tightly that there was no water left in it. "What is wrong now?" I asked, and we discussed the problems of squeezing too much water out. Next, I showed her the correct way to wring the cloth and showed her how to mop so that the entire floor was covered. These few minutes invested in proper training solved the mopping problem.

Likewise, when we plant the little seeds in our garden in early spring, each of the older children is responsible for watering two or three rows. We have shown them the correct procedure for watering—a small stream of water trickling over the newly planted seeds as the hose is moved slowly back and forth over the rows. If the children had only been shown *what* to do without explaining *why*, they may assume that by turning the water on twice as much, they could get done twice as fast—and unintentionally wash away all those little seeds. Or, they may hold the hose too long in one place, causing erosion—hence, the necessity of discussing the *how* and *why* of *what* you do in order to avoid mistakes and misunderstandings.

Caleb irrigates. Speaking of gardens, we have a never-to-be-forgotten story illustrating the need for specific explanations when delegating tasks. It was our turn to irrigate, and Caleb was helping his dad.

By way of explanation, Utah is carved into miles of irrigation ditches, enabling water stored in mountain reservoirs to water crops and fields of this desert landscape during the hot summer months. A system of weirs and headgates channels water to the correct location, each person opening their own headgate at the beginning of their irrigation turn and closing it at the end to allow the water to flow on to the next person.

On this particular day, my husband got Caleb started early in the morning, then left for work, telling him to be sure to close the headgate when our turn was over. At the appointed time, however, Caleb, noticing that our ditch was beginning to empty, assumed that the next person had taken the water and felt no need to close our gate.

Later in the day, I noticed water puddling in the field; but as that was a fairly common occurrence on irrigation day, I didn't think much about it. It wasn't until Camille went out to water our newly-planted garden around four o'clock that we realized we had a problem. A steady stream of water was flowing into the garden from the irrigation ditch. In the past, we never had enough irrigation water to get down to our garden; and I immediately quizzed my son about closing the headgate.

He explained that he had not closed it because the water in the ditch looked like it was going down. Only now did he see the error of his decision, and he promptly ran to close it. Even with the gate closed, however, water continued to flow into the garden for two more hours as the ditch continued to empty. Our efforts to divert the water were futile, and we ended up with a garden almost completely covered with several inches of standing water.

It was nearly two days before the water finally soaked into the ground and at least another week before the ground dried out completely. We worried about the tender tomato and pepper plants and whether the seeds in the ground had been washed away or would even sprout. All we could do was wait.

To make matters worse, Utah was experiencing a three-year drought; water was at a premium. In our little community, we were surrounded by farmers whose livelihood depended on every precious drop of water. We felt guilty about our seeming extravagance. Located alongside the road, our garden was easily visible to passersby, and I lived in dread of being reported for some sort of water conservation violation.

Luckily, this story has a happy ending. We were never accused of any crimes and, miraculously, the new little plants survived and even the seeds sprouted. The potatoes, however, came in poorly; and we ended up replanting some of them. To our surprise, we had a very productive garden that year.

Furthermore, Caleb learned an important lesson about following directions even if you don't understand why. And my husband learned an important lesson about discussing with your children *why* they do *what* they do.

Jarom washes an onion. Another example of the need for clear directions occurred as I was revising this very section. When the baby started crying, I walked into the kitchen to get her just as my eight-year-old son was preparing to peel an onion for a Dutch oven meal my husband was "fixing", which means that several of the children were also in the kitchen—scrubbing, peeling, stirring . . . but we've already discussed all that.

Anyway, my son was at the kitchen sink washing an onion he had pulled from the garden. My husband walked to the sink just in time to see him dip the onion in the warm, soapy dish water. "Don't wash it like that!" he scolded. "You don't wash onions in soapy water." And then in a more apologetic tone, he added, "But I guess I didn't clarify that when I asked you to wash the onion."

"This is perfect," I bellowed. "I was just revising the section on never assuming anything and always discussing the *what, why,* and *how* when assigning tasks."

Embarrassed, my son hung his head. I tried to encourage him by saying, "Don't feel bad, Jarom. This will make a great story for my book."

I think you get the point! It's such a simple thing, but it's easy to forget or to assume that some things don't need an explanation. Children need more. They do not have the benefit of wisdom that comes with age and experience. What may be clearly obvious to you, may not be at all obvious to them. You can help them avoid many mistakes with a few minutes of explanation.

The Fifth "D": Discipline— "The Greatest Firmness is the Greatest Mercy"

Discipline is the most important aspect of delegation; it will make or break the whole delegation process. Without discipline, delegation is merely a lofty ideal. Ideally, children should work out of a sense of duty, love for their parents, or a sense of belonging in the family; but, as you well know, we do not live in an ideal world. Therefore, children must be taught responsibility. For discussion purposes, I have separated discipline into three areas:

- **Accountability**
- **Consequences**
- **Consistency**

Accountability

Accountability is an absolute. When we think of delegation, we often focus on the process of making assignments and providing adequate training, often overlooking the most important step—accountability. Accountability means that children are personally responsible for their assigned tasks; and when they fail to complete them, there will be some sort of consequence. It is really a pretty simple concept, but it can be difficult to enforce. It takes time, lots of time, and effort, lots of effort. It can be mentally, emotionally, and physically draining; but it is, nevertheless, vital to successful delegation.

Many frustrated parents bemoan the fact that their children will not cooperate. Some of them have had family councils, some have taken the time to train their children, and some have even gone to the trouble of making elaborate job charts. But, all too soon, the enthusiasm wears off, and they find that nothing is getting done. The parent is then left wondering, "Where did I go wrong?" The secret is accountability.

That which is reported on, gets done. There needs to be some kind of follow-up plan. Children need to know that someone will be checking their work, not only to see that it is done in a timely fashion but that it is done well. They must know that if either is found lacking, there will be consequences; and they must be willing to accept the consequences of their own actions or lack thereof. In simplest terms, accountability means that you hold your children responsible for their responsibilities.

Consequences

Every behavior has a consequence. This thought is prominently displayed on our refrigerator. It is a gentle reminder to the children that they are free to choose their behavior, but they are not free from the consequences of their choices. They understand, too, that there are good and bad consequences depending on their behavior.

At our home, when the little ones are disobedient, we usually sit them on a chair for a few minutes to give them time to think about what they have done wrong. Before they can get off the chair, we give them a "talk". During this talk, we discuss what they did or did not do and what they could or should have done instead and how they can improve in the future. We also point out that in the time they have been sitting on a chair they could have had the assigned task completed. Instead, they have spent their time sitting on a chair, and now they still have to do their job. We end with a few words of encouragement and a hug.

For our older children the consequences are more involved. We have found that assigning an extra task to the one already assigned is very effective—washing walls, washing windows, cleaning a drawer, or straightening a closet. This kills two birds with one stone—the child gets disciplined *and* I get some of those neglected projects completed!

Some mothers have wondered whether using work as punishment won't cause children to dislike work. We have not found this to be the case in our home. What it does help them realize is that it is much better to do the first job in a timely manner to avoid having extra work. Furthermore, we usually assign them tasks that no one really likes doing anyway. And your approach as a parent can make a difference in their attitude as well.

Be sure your children understand that consequences are a direct result of choices *they* have made. It's a great way to teach the principle of choice and accountability. This can be done simply, directly, calmly, and lovingly by saying something like: "I'm sorry you didn't mow the lawn last night. I guess you chose to wash windows today." You can even add a bit of humor: "I see you didn't do the dishes. That's so nice of you to volunteer to wash a wall. I've got one that's really dirty!"

If they protest, remind them of the family council where you discussed and agreed upon acceptable consequences. Express your love for them. It is important for them to know that you care about them as a person but are disappointed in their behavior. Be sure to stress the fact that *they* made the decision not to obey; and by so doing, *they* made the decision to accept the consequences that accompany that disobedience. This puts the responsibility back on them, and then they can only be mad at themselves.

Don't feel guilty; you're not the bad guy. I am reminded of a scene in the movie *Dennis the Menace* where Mr. Wilson is ranting and raving about what a terrible son Mr. Mitchell has and that Dennis is no longer welcome to visit. As Mr. Mitchell drives away, Mr. Wilson hollers after him, "I'm not the bad guy in this Mitchell, I'm the victim!" So it is with your children. Don't let them make *you* out to be the bad guy when they are disciplined for *their* disobedience.

This is especially important for mothers to remember. We tend to be more soft-hearted and sympathetic. Too often we give in rather than see our children "suffer". I know. I have a problem with this myself. I tend to nag and nag, giving them several chances rather than face the problem head on. What usually happens is that I get all worked up. The volume of my voice escalates along with my blood pressure, creating more stress and tension for myself than necessary. The repeated nagging only teaches my children that they don't need to mind me the first time, creating a habit of disobedience.

My husband is much better, and I have learned much from watching him. When he asks a child to do something and discovers later that it hasn't been done, he says calmly, almost in a whisper, "Go sit on a chair." There is no anger, no stress, no escalating tension. I marvel at how easy he makes it look.

The consequence must fit the crime and the criminal. Being too lenient engenders indifference, while being too harsh begets resentment and rebellion. Often, when I find my child goofing off when he should be working, I will say something like, "You have five minutes to start on the dishes or there's going to be trouble;" or "If I come back in fifteen minutes and your bed isn't made, there are going to be consequences."

The child is then left to wonder, "What kind of consequences?" "What kind of trouble?" Perhaps he may even imagine something far worse than I had in mind, which will be enough to get him moving. This vague, ambiguous threat also gives me time to cool off a bit while I think of an appropriate consequence—one that hasn't been hastily uttered in the heat of the moment.

I can't tell you how many times I have gone to my room and rocked back and forth in my chair while thinking about appropriate consequences for a disobedient child. Sometimes I am so angry, I want to lash out with something really harsh—something, by the way, that I will probably regret later. As I rock and ponder, rock and ponder, I am able to think more rationally. Finally, after a sufficient cooling-down period and some careful reflection, I am able to come up with an appropriate consequence.

"Never use a cannon when a water pistol will do."[3] Avoid rash, unrealistic threats such as, "You're not going to the party tonight!" or "You're grounded for a week!" (I have even heard one mother say, "You're grounded for a month!") Unless, of course, you feel it is justified and you are willing to stick with it. Remember, when you discipline, you are the one who must carry it out. Make sure it is something you can live with, too! Once the discipline has been issued, stay firm. Don't back down or turn soft. And don't give in to whining and pleading and promises to never do it again.

One day my ten-year-old, Trenton, had been especially disobedient. As a last resort, I gave him an ultimatum: start cooperating or he wouldn't be able to play with friends that afternoon. He didn't heed my warning, and I finally told him he couldn't play. A few hours later, he had two phone calls from two different friends inviting him to play. Time had passed, things had settled down, and my feelings of frustration were gone. Even though I knew the initial punishment was justified, I desperately wanted to let him play. But I also knew that if I relented, my future attempts at discipline would be greatly diminished. This was definitely one of those times when the punishment hurt me

---

3. *Children Who Do Too Little,* Patricia H. Sprinkle, Zondervan Publishing House, Grand Rapids, MI, 1996, p. 126.

more than it did him. Even the most well-deserved discipline can be difficult to enforce, especially on a long-term basis—hence, the need for carefully considered, reasonable consequences. (That may involve a lot of rocking!).

Discipline need not be long term in order to be successful. For this very reason, I do not like grounding. I feel it is used too frequently and too often inappropriately. It seems to be the cure-all for most of the problems we encounter with our children. Generally, grounding is difficult to enforce with the passage of time and the cooling of tempers. Three days later, your child is still being disciplined for not making his bed; and he has a hard time making the connection.

Something firm and prompt is much better. Perhaps that is why the "extra job" approach is so effective. The child does his job, the discipline is complete, and you move on with life.

As much as possible, the punishment should be a logical consequence of their disobedience. For example, one of our daughters was having trouble getting her bed made before school in the morning. After this had happened several days, and after adequate warning, my husband pulled off all her bedding, and told her to remake the entire bed. She was then told that the next time her bed wasn't made, the same thing would happen. It only took once for her to realize that it was much easier to spend a few extra minutes making her bed *before* school rather than remaking the entire bed *after* school, and it was a long time before she forgot to make it again.

Another time, I was having trouble with one of the children putting her clothes in the laundry inside out. This happened for several weeks and was considerable effort on my part to turn them right side out. When my requests for her help in the matter got me no where, I finally told her if it happened again she would wash those clothes by hand. Apparently, she didn't take me seriously because the very next week several items of clothing were turned inside out. I set them aside for her to wash by hand that very evening. Interestingly enough, I haven't had any problem since!

Negative and Positive Motivation. The consequences mentioned above are forms of negative motivation—a child does something wrong and something unpleasant happens. Of course, positive motivation—a thank you, a hug, a compliment, an occasional reward—is by far the better choice. However, when a child is especially rebellious or consistently disobedient and all else fails, as it surely will from time to time despite our best efforts, then stronger action must be taken (*My Children Refuse to Work,* 77-80).

Consequence is the inseparable companion of choice. It is important for children to learn that as they sow, so shall they reap. They need to understand the law of consequences; life is full of them. Failure to allow them to experience the natural consequences of their behavior only prolongs the inevitable, making the eventual discovery that much more difficult. They need to understand that to a large degree *they* are responsible for their own happiness or misery depending on *their* obedience or disobedience.

Consistency

Consistency is crucial. To be effective, consequences must be applied as consistently as possible. Children must know there will be consequences for disobedience. It doesn't take them long to learn whether or not you mean what you say. When they realize you are serious, they are more apt to obey. However, if they know that you regularly go back on your word or that you rarely follow through, they are more willing to take risks about being disobedient, hoping they get lucky. Repeated threats without action become hollow and meaningless.

A few years ago, I was having a problem with my younger boys doing what I asked them to do—simple things like making their beds and dumping garbage. I kept getting after them—nagging, scolding, threatening; but they didn't cooperate. At last it dawned on me that I was not being consistent in issuing consequences when they disobeyed. "Something has got to change," I decided. "I need to be more firm. They need to know that I mean business." So I settled on a course of action and began the new program.

The next day I asked four-year-old Abram to make his bed. When I came back a while later and discovered that he had not done a thing, I said, "Abram, look at me" (I learned from a friend years ago that making eye contact increases the probability that they're listening). When he looked at me I said, "I want you to make your bed. If I come back and you're not doing it, there are going to be consequences."

He immediately threw himself on a chair, whining in a disgusted, pouty voice, "Mom, you have to give me a billion chances!"

"No, you don't get a billion chances," I replied, "you get one."

I was tightening up, and he didn't like it. It took a while for my boys to get used to our new way of doing things, but they eventually caught on that I was serious; and things got much better.

Consistency between parents is also important. It is important that both parents make the effort to follow through with discipline. Children are quick to pick up on any discrepancies between parents. They know which parent is more lenient and will play you against each other if you let them. Therefore, it is important to be in agreement about what chores will be done, who will do them, and consequences for not getting them done. Do not contradict each other in front of the children. Any disagreements should be discussed in private, approaching the children only after the two of you have reached a mutually acceptable consensus.

Hang in there. I've got to say that some days can really be draining, especially with young children. Some days you feel that they spend more time on a chair than not and that you spend most of your time disciplining. It does get better. Trust me! If you can hang in there until they get over the hump of their learning curve, it will eventually register in their developing minds that it is much better to obey. In time, there will be less nagging, less scolding, less threatening and more cooperation. It really is a much better way.

The Sixth "D": Determination

You can do it! I'll be the first to admit that delegation is not easy. It is not a one-time effort and then you're done. It requires a lot of effort today, and then you wake up tomorrow and start all over again. It is a daily ongoing battle; and, honestly, some days I wonder why I even try. One day the children will be excellent, cooperative workers. The next day they're silly and ornery, and it's a struggle all day to get them moving. And, you know, it really isn't fun trying to get children to do things they really don't want to do. Sometimes I feel like I'm pushing water up hill with a rake. You will experience failures, but keep trying! As they say, success is getting up each time you fall down.

Go ahead and cry! . . . or take a long walk, a hot bath, or count to ten—whatever it is you do to relieve stress. If you think it's bad trying to get one or two or three or four children to work, try ten! Some days it is just too much. I feel like Alexander in the popular children's book who is having a "terrible, horrible, no good, very bad day."[4] I am a volcano ready to erupt. When I get too overwhelmed, I have found that a fast bike ride or a few minutes weeding in the yard can be very therapeutic. Sometimes,

---

4. *Alexander and the Terrible, Horrible, No Good, Very Bad Day,* Judith Viorst, Aladdin Books, New York, NY, 1987.

though, I fling myself on the bed and let it all out in a good cry. All the stress, all the frustration, all the anger seems to come out through my tears; and in fifteen or twenty minutes, I'm ready to face the children again.

By the way, there has been some interesting research on tears. "Tears cleanse your mind and soul of stresses, strains, and frustrations. . . . [They] are as potent as laughter when it comes to physical and psychological relief. Crying provides an emotional release that can lower blood pressure and reduce emotional and muscle tension."[5]

One day was particularly bad. It was laundry day, and there had been more loads than usual. When my daughter got home from school, I asked her to hang a load outside on the clothesline. She told me "no", muttering something about why did *she* have to do it and why wasn't anyone else working. I ignored her comments, hoping she would give in without a confrontation.

An hour later she still had not done it, and it was now time for piano lessons. I asked her in a firm, don't-you-dare-say-no voice if she would please hang the clothes before we had to leave in ten minutes. She grumbled angrily, "Where are the clothes?" (Like this was her first day doing laundry.)

Annoyed with her attitude, I grumbled back, "Where do you think the clothes are?" At which point, she stomped off to the laundry room. While she hung the clothes, I finished up a few loose ends, all the while uptight about leaving in time for piano lessons since we also needed to pick up my son on the way.

When my daughter didn't come in as soon as I expected, I decided to grab the clothes out of the dryer and take them to my room so they would be ready to fold when I returned. However, upon opening the dryer, I discovered it was empty. My first

---

5. Hope Health Letter, July 2004, Vol. 24, No. 7.

thought was that my daughter may have already taken them to my room. But, then, my second more incredulous thought was that perhaps she was at that very moment outside hanging them on the line. (Impossible!) A quick check of the washing machine with the wet clothes still inside confirmed my suspicions.

Now fuming with irritation, I hollered outside for her to take the clothes off the line and bring them back inside, which she did. When she came in, I ranted something about what in the world she thought she was doing and where did she think the clothes would be that should be hung outside, all the while throwing wet clothes into the basket. I then told her to go back outside and hang the wet clothes on the line and to hurry because we were now late for piano lessons.

I finished up a few more little projects while waiting for her to come in, but she didn't come. Fifteen minutes later, she was still hanging clothes and seemed to be deliberately making it take longer than necessary, so I decided to leave without her. By now I was so angry, I could spit fire.

It was a good thing I had a twenty minute trip to piano because it took me that long to cool down. All the way, I was thinking of appropriate consequences. It had to be something significant enough to make up for her difficulty with chores *and* for missing piano lessons. I decided she would work for the next two hours—washing walls and helping with dinner.

When I got home, I had cooled off enough to discuss the problem in a civil tone. We talked about her disobedience when I had initially asked her to hang clothes. I pointed out that the problem wouldn't have been nearly as bad had she done it an hour earlier when there would have still been time to fix it without being late for piano. I also told her what the consequences would be. She knew better than complain this time!

My younger boys didn't make the day any better. Before I left for piano, I had told my younger boys to clean up their toys and be prepared to help when I returned. Just as I walked in the back door, I saw two of the boys walking across the back lawn toward the swing. I called to them, and then went about my work. Apparently, they hadn't heard me—or pretended not to hear. When I realized they had not come in, I called them again, asking them to cut up a melon. I then went to my room to put the baby to sleep. They cut up the melon and immediately ran back outside to play. I returned to find them gone and the melon—that was to be for dinner—mostly eaten!

Once again, I called to them, asking them to get the clothes off the line. It was my plan to ask for more help when they brought the clothes in. However, they outsmarted me by sending four-year-old Levi in with the clothes who dropped them off at the top of the stairs and ran back outside.

When I called them again, I was not very happy. This time I asked them to set the table which they quickly did. And, *again,* they were off, scattering throughout the house in several directions— anywhere to avoid getting caught by Mom to do more work.

Once more, I called them together and explained sternly that I needed their help and that I expected them all to stay where they would be available to help. It was like trying to catch baby chicks. As soon as I caught one, the rest ran away. "Why does it have to be so hard?" I lamented. "Why can't they just stick around and be helpful?"

When I had time to think about it later, I realized it was mostly my fault. I kept asking them to do one thing which they obediently did and then scampered off, assuming they were fin- ished. Had I brought them together initially, explaining every- thing that needed to be done, they would have known exactly what was expected; and I wouldn't have had near the trouble.

Determination was the only thing that kept me going that day— determination to teach my children in spite of their lack of interest in learning and determination to endure despite the challenges.

Humor can be a great stress reliever. I know it's nearly impossible at times, but try to see the humor in the hubbub that surrounds you. Step back from the situation a little. Call a friend. Write in your journal. (You'll laugh about it later.) At the end of some days, I entertain my husband with the day's events. Somehow when I'm rehearsing to him the chaos and confusion of the day, it can actually be funny—even hilarious.

Other times it isn't so funny. Sometimes I complain bitterly how so and so did this and so and so wouldn't do that and how there was grumbling and complaining and fighting and sloppy work. He listens politely. Then, with a wry smile and a quizzical look, he's been known to say, "Didn't you write a book about this?"

Nodding my head dismally, I respond (sometimes through tears), "Yes . . . yes, I did . . . but it's a lot easier said than done."

Theory and reality can be miles apart. Sometimes I fail miserably. The basic philosophy is not hard, but the daily grind can get to be a challenge. I have had enough successes, though, to know that theory and reality occasionally do converge. It is for those times that I continue to persist. I am determined to stick with it in spite of the challenges and difficulties for my children's sake and for the good that I believe will eventually come of it.

3

ELIMINATING POSSIBLE STUMBLING BLOCKS TO YOUR SUCCESS

In idleness there is perpetual despair.
—Thomas Carlyle

Most parents, I believe, understand the value of work and really do want their children to do more around the house. It is certainly not a lack of desire that keeps us from teaching our children to work. Most often, it is a lack of knowledge about how and where to start, which we have just addressed. Furthermore, on any given day, we may encounter stumbling blocks that prevent us from being as effective as possible in our efforts to delegate.

We try to do too much. We feel sorry for our children. I know I did when I first started, and I still struggle with that feeling even today. Sometimes without even realizing it, we make excuses for our children and ourselves that get in the way of helping our children become what we really want them to become. Perhaps you have encountered some of these stumbling blocks yourself:

Misplaced Focus:

- I can do it faster myself.
- If you want it done right, do it yourself.
- I find it enjoyable.
- I'm a creature of habit.

- I feel sorry for them.
- They don't do it my way.
- I'm starting too late in their lives.
- My children aren't capable.

Resistance from Your Children:

- My children are too busy.
- My children complain.
- Some children work better than others.
- My children refuse to work.
- My teenagers are intolerable.
- My children expect to get paid.

Delegation is hard enough without any unnecessary obstacles. In the sections that follow, I will address each stumbling block,[1] discussing the underlying principles and possible remedies. Hopefully, you will find solutions that will assist you in your efforts at successful delegation.

"I Can Do It Faster Myself"

Principle—The greatest investment you can give your child is your time.

I would expect that you could do it faster yourself. You've had many years to refine and hone your skills. Think back to the first time *you* tried to clean the bathtub, mop the floor, or make a batch of cookies. How long did it take?

---

1. *Delegate,* Harold L. Taylor, Warner Books, Inc., New York, NY, 1989, pp. 28-33, 79-86. Contains further information on delegation.

I can still remember the first time I made lasagna as a teenage girl. It took all day. I did each step separately and consecutively. It didn't occur to me that I could cook the noodles *while* I fried the hamburger. That one meal was a major event, and I can still remember wondering how my mom did it all.

Even as a new bride it took longer to do my work than it does today. I've learned a few tricks over the years. I've learned to work faster and smarter. In fact, I've learned—or rather, been forced to learn—to do fifteen things at once.

When you first begin to delegate, you may not notice immediate results. In fact, initially, delegation may create more stress and take more of your time, especially if you have young children. The first time you assign a task, you will need to show the child *what* to do and *how* to do it while discussing *why* you do it. The next few times, depending on the job that needs to be completed and the age and capacity of the child, you may need to show them again or at least be available to answer questions and check their work. Soon enough, though, they will be able to perform the task easily and without assistance; and that's when the payoff *finally* comes. In the meantime, remember patience, patience, patience.

Stay nearby. In order to avoid a lot of frustration during this training phase, I have found it easier to work near the child, occupying myself with simple projects that don't take a lot of concentration. If I am engrossed in deep cleaning the basement, I will become agitated with continual interruptions, especially if I have to keep traipsing upstairs. However, by planning work that can be easily interrupted, I can lend assistance with a much more cheerful attitude, thereby making it a more pleasant experience for everyone involved.

In spite of their inexperience, two or three children working together can actually complete a task much faster than you could by yourself. Many hands make light work. Take the laundry, for example. It would take me quite some time to match a week's worth of socks for a family of twelve; but when everyone helps, the pile disappears in minutes.

With my first seven children I used cloth diapers. It took approximately twenty minutes to fold five dozen diapers myself. However, when several of the children worked together, it went much faster. In fact, they liked to have races to see how quickly they could finish. The record was one minute, forty-five seconds! There is no way I could have ever done it that quickly myself.

At the risk of being redundant, let me emphasize again: be patient. Speed is not everything. Your children are parents in training, and your home is their training ground. A little investment of your time now will reap immeasurable rewards in the years to come.

"If You Want It Done Right, Do It Yourself"

Principle—You get what you expect.

If you expect little, you'll get little. Most children know just what they can get away with and will perform at that level. You set the standard.

Basically, there are three reasons a child is not performing at your desired expectations: capacity, poor training, or lack of accountability. In this section we will discuss the first two reasons; accountability has already been discussed (*Discipline*, 34-42).

"Nothing comes from nothing. Nothing ever will" (Richard Rogers). In other words, you've got to let your children practice if they're ever going to get any better. If a child is incapable of performing a task as well as you would like, be patient. Success will come in time, but you must be willing to accept less than perfection when they first start taking on new assignments.

Naturally, it is frustrating when you find patches of grass that have been missed by the mower, dirty spots on a supposedly clean kitchen floor, or grit and smudges on the just-cleaned bathroom sink. It goes without saying that in the beginning the work will probably not be done as well as you could do it. Show them, guide them, be available to lend assistance and answer questions; but remember, they're just learning. Be *patient* with their awkwardness and their delay; be willing to *tolerate* less than you would from yourself or from an older, more experienced child.

For your little ones, the results are not as important as the process. One day while refinishing some antique wooden chairs, two-year-old Levi got a piece of sandpaper and enthusiastically tried to do his part. We all praised him and commented on how cute he looked. He worked steadily for quite some time before one of the children finally noticed that he had the sandpaper upside down! Even though he wasn't really making any significant contribution, his accomplishments were not nearly as important as his perception of what he was doing. He *felt* important and helpful; and he was learning that when the family worked, we all worked.

"But my children are capable," you may be saying, "but still they do not perform as well as I would like." If this is the case, the problem could be a training problem. Be sure they know exactly what you want done, how to do it (proper training), and why it must be done a specific way (*Be Specific,* 21-22, and *Demonstrate,* 30-34).

If you ask your seven-year-old to clean the bathroom sink, and he doesn't do it right, whose fault is it? Sometimes we blame the child when the problem is the result of poor training. Never *assume* that your child knows how to do a task.

Too often I have asked a child to do something only to discover sometime later, usually when they are half finished with the project, that they aren't doing it at all like I expected. Most of the time I realize that I didn't spend any time explaining exactly what I wanted done and how. A few moments of explanation at the outset would save us both a lot of frustration.

If you ask your child to turn the outside sprinkler off, don't *assume* she is going to roll up the hose and put the sprinkler away, too. (Even if she's seen you do it that way a hundred times.) And, if you tell her to put the sprinkler away, don't assume she will put it away where it belongs. But, if you say, "Please turn the water off, roll up the hose, and put the sprinkler away where it goes," then you can expect things to be done properly.

Expect the best they can give, but also accept the best they can give. Do your part to ensure success by providing adequate training, but at the same time, be willing to tolerate less than perfection, especially with your little ones. Tolerance, however, does not mean accepting intentional sloppiness. If you know your child is capable of more, if he did better last week, if he is angry about doing the work or in a hurry to play with friends, make him do the job again. Have him rewash dirty dishes or redo the bathroom floor if it isn't clean. You may even need to call them home from playing with their friends to redo work that isn't acceptable, but it probably won't happen too often.

If *you* are consistent, they will soon learn it is easier to do it right the first time. Once they know what your expectations are, they will perform at that level. Keep your standards high.

"I Find It Enjoyable"

Principle—If you keep all the plums for yourself, the only thing left for others is the pits.

Maybe you really do enjoy housework or yard work—some people do. However, by freeing yourself from some of these tasks, or at least shortening the time for their completion, you will have time for other things that you may enjoy even more. Besides, the ultimate goal, remember, is to provide opportunities for work and growth for our children, thereby teaching them responsibility while simultaneously raising their self-esteem.

Pass on your love of work to your children. I know one mother who loves flowers. She plants hundreds of seeds in little containers in February so they will be ready for planting in spring. However, she never lets her children work in the flower beds. How unfortunate. Not only are her children missing out on important work experiences, but they are also missing out on incredible opportunities to glean knowledge from their mother as they work beside her. And, who knows, perhaps in the process she could pass on to them her love of gardening.

Be careful not to delegate only the trivial, mundane tasks. Let children do those things they may perceive as fun or grown up—operating the tiller, mixing the bread, waxing the car, or frosting the cake. Sometimes there is a tendency to reserve a few "pet" projects for ourselves.

I enjoy cake decorating (or at least I used to), and for many years I went to great effort to make elaborately decorated cakes for my children's birthdays. I would spend the better part of an afternoon mixing frosting and making flowers and fancy borders. While I took great pride in the finished product, the task was time consuming and stressful with several children huddled around trying to "watch." (They had a hard time understanding that you see with your eyes, not your fingers.) As the number of children increased, along with the demands on my time, I found cake decorating less and less interesting. One year, when I was particularly busy, I decided to let my three boys with November birthdays decorate their own cakes. My boys were thrilled with the idea and had a great time decorating with candy corn and gum drops. In fact, they enjoyed it so much that it became a new tradition in our home—one which has freed up some of my time and which is rewarding and enjoyable for the children.

Delegate something you may find enjoyable for something you may discover to be even more enjoyable. It may be something as noteworthy as pursuing a college degree or starting your own business. Or, it may be as simple as having time to enjoy life's little pleasures: reading a book, going for a walk, enjoying a sunset, or—heaven forbid—taking a nap.

"I'm a Creature of Habit"

Principle—If you always do what you've always done, you'll always get what you've always got.

Habits can be broken. After all, flexibility is the first rule of delegation. This is when the first two steps of delegation become so important. (*Decide* 23-24, and *Divide* 24-27.) Make a list of all your chores, then ask yourself, "Could the children be doing any of these tasks?" If so, in consultation with your family, divide the jobs among the various members.

One mother, upon deciding that her children could now do more, asked her son to do a job that he was not accustomed to doing. When he protested indignantly, "That's not my job," she responded simply, "It is now."

Take time to sharpen the saw. There I am—running around crazy with a dozen things to do, all of which need my immediate attention. And there are my children—reading, riding bikes, playing games, chasing through the house. Because I am so caught up in my own dilemma, I forget to take advantage of the great potential source of help that literally surrounds me. It may take a few minutes to stop, analyze the situation and marshall the resources of my children; but in the end, it will save a lot of time, energy, and stress.

Be aware of those spontaneous tasks that could be assigned to one of the children—scrubbing potatoes, peeling carrots, dressing a younger child, straightening a shelf, setting the table. Each of these tasks may only take a few minutes, but in those few minutes you could accomplish other tasks that the children may not be able to do. For example, in the time you spend scrubbing potatoes, you could have gone through the day's mail, cleaned off a counter, sorted through a stack of papers, or written a birthday card or a thank you note. When combined, these "little" projects produce big results in your overall feeling of accomplishment.

Notwithstanding the many little things children can do to be helpful, I must point out that I don't spend my days running to find a child every time there's a task to do. If I spend ten minutes getting someone to do a five-minute job, my efforts are actually counterproductive. And, sometimes when all the children are playing happily outside or are busy with quiet projects around the house, I'm perfectly content to let them be. Sometimes the peace and quiet is worth the extra work I may have to do myself. *But,* if there's fighting or teasing or chasing through the house, you can be sure that I'll find something for them to do.

Force yourself to think of new ways to do things. This may mean changing your schedule or rearranging the way you're used to doing things. Just because you've cleaned the bathrooms at 10:00 a.m. on Monday for years, doesn't mean they couldn't get just as clean on Thursday at 3:00. We tend to function better on a schedule, so it's easy to get into a routine or to develop a certain mindset about how things *should* be done around the house. I can tell you from personal experience that you can learn to do things another way that will be equally satisfactory.

When my older children were young, I liked to clean house first thing in the morning, doing the major chores while I was ambitious and had more energy. However, when I started home-schooling, I soon realized that those early morning hours were also the best time for teaching the children, capturing their minds while they were still fresh and alert and ready to learn. Consequently, housework soon took a back seat to school. I learned, in spite of my preconceived bias, that it is possible to mop floors, vacuum, and clean the bathroom in the afternoon. I spent the morning hours doing school with the children. In return, they helped me clean house in the afternoon.

A few years later, when the older children started going to public school and their afternoons were filled with homework, I again analyzed the housecleaning situation and decided we would do the majority of the housecleaning on Saturday, allowing the children more time to focus on their studies during the week.

Although I mention these changes in routine rather casually, I can assure you that they definitely took some getting use to. The house was not always as clean as I would have liked; but under the circumstances, it was the best solution. After the initial adjustment phase, however, the new schedule became the accepted routine and life went on quite satisfactorily.

Catch yourself doing things you shouldn't. As I stooped to pick up yet another toy lying carelessly on the floor, the thought came to me, "As long as you keep picking up their toys, you'll always be picking them up." Children are happy to let you do as much as you will for them. If you always pick up their toys, put away their clothes, or clean up the bathroom after them, you'll be doing it forever. Stop. Ask yourself if you have created a habit; if so, make the necessary changes.

Flexibility is the first rule of delegation. Change is inevitable. Be prepared and willing to accept it.

"I'm Not Organized Enough"

Principle—The more you delegate, the more time you have to organize; and the more organized you become, the easier it is to delegate.

Getting organized is a never-ending battle. To be honest, I don't know that it is actually possible to be completely organized with small children. It seems as soon as I get one thing cleaned up, something else is a mess. I can't tell you how many times I clean off my kitchen counter every week. And, as soon as I do, the kids come home with papers or the mail comes; and before I know it, it's all cluttered again. Someone once told me that "cleaning the house while your kids are still growing is like shoveling the walk while it is still snowing."

I certainly don't claim to be an expert in this area. The truth is that I have a lot of ideas for getting organized, but implementing them is another story. However, there are a few things I have found to be helpful in maintaining some degree of sanity.

Keep a day planner of some sort. It need not be elaborate or expensive. (I use the $5 generic kind.) In addition to keeping track of appointments and activities, use your planner to keep track of the little things that so often slip through the cracks: mending a shirt, writing a thank you card, making a phone call, cleaning a drawer. How many times have you noticed something that needs to be done and thought to yourself, "When so and so gets get home, I'm going to have him clean his dresser, straighten that drawer, or sweep the porch." Then, a few days later, you notice the same unfinished project and realize you never asked anyone to do it. That's what your planner is for— to keep track of the little tasks that need to be completed. It's hard to delegate if you don't even remember the things that need to be delegated. A planner also helps plan the sequence of tasks to be completed, thus helping to make the most efficient use of your time. If you waste fifteen minutes a day, that's two weeks of lost time a year.[2] Imagine what you could do with an extra two weeks!

Make lists. I keep a shopping list in my kitchen. Actually, there are several lists. There is a separate page for groceries, home improvement, bulk shopping (Sam's, Costco), and variety shopping (WalMart, K-Mart). The entire family knows they are there and how to use them. When they open the last jar or can or box of something, they are to write that item on the shopping list. The idea is that when I go shopping, I can get everything I need in one trip. (Assuming everything was written on the list in the first place.) Other lists are also helpful: mending to be done, projects to complete, odd jobs for the children. Keeping lists clears your head of a lot of clutter.

Go to bed with a clean house. This doesn't mean immaculate from floor to ceiling, but at least gather up all the toys (even if you just stack them in a corner of the room), wash the dishes, straighten the kitchen, and have children pick up their clothes and toys in their bedrooms.

When we lived on the North Shore of Oahu, Hawaii, we were 45-60 minutes from the major shopping centers in our area, so "going to town" was quite an ordeal. Once a month, we ran all our errands, stopping at several stores along the way. By the time we returned from our shopping trip, it was about 9:00 p.m. Tired after a long day, we unloaded the van, put away the perishables, and left the rest until morning. I dreaded going into the kitchen the next morning. Before the day even began, I was off to a bad start. Going to bed with your house in a general sense of order will make a tremendous difference in how you feel the next day.

---

2. *Delegate,* Harold L. Taylor, Warner Books, New York, NY, 1989, p. 54.

I have found it much easier to keep the house clean if we have periodic clean ups throughout the day—a clean up before lunch, a quick clean up before leaving the house for any extended period of time, one at dinner, and another at bedtime. Leo D. Bardsley has wisely said, "It is so much easier to keep up than catch up."

Have a plan for the next day. "Psychologists claim we enjoy our evening and weekend pursuits a lot more when we leave the office with an organized desk and a plan for the next day."[3] This is true of our homes as well. Doing little things the night before can make a big difference in getting off to a good start the next morning: putting the dishes away, mixing orange juice, or getting bread out of the freezer. (If we even have any bread in the freezer.) You can get going much more quickly in the morning if things are in order when you wake up and you have a plan for the day.

Make the most of the minutes. Take advantage of those short, unexpected time periods that occur throughout the day as discussed in the previous section. Get your children doing more. Find ways of gaining an extra ten or fifteen minutes here and there. It's amazing what can be accomplished in just a few minutes of concentrated effort.

With ten children, I consider it a miracle if I have more than fifteen uninterrupted minutes. If I waited for extensive blocks of time to pursue lengthy projects, I would never accomplish anything. I made curtains for my kitchen in twenty to thirty minute time segments, maybe an hour when I was lucky. We refinished our wooden chairs over a period of two months, working only thirty to forty minutes a day. And this book has primarily been written in brief, sporadic, unpredictable time snatches, with the exception of those wonderful evenings when my dear husband

---

3. *Delegate,* Harold L. Taylor, Warner Books, New York, NY, 1989, p. 48.

runs the household so I can lock myself away for a few hours of quiet time.

Finally, don't expect to organize everything all at once. The very thought is overwhelming. A marathon is not run in one giant leap but in small, persistent steps one after the other. Likewise, the key to achievement in our lives is not found in great blocks of uninterrupted time but rather in short, steady, consistent efforts. Think small. Make a plan. Set a goal. Just for today you can straighten a drawer, organize a closet, or clean a room. Bit by bit, room by room, success can be realized.

"I Feel Sorry for Them"

Principle—"Hard work never killed a man, but it sure has scared a lot of them."

Don't feel sorry for them! You're not hurting your children at all by making them work. On the contrary, learning to work will be one of the greatest blessings of their lives. Through work, they will learn responsibility, accountability, and dependability while simultaneously raising their self-esteem. The children you really should feel sorry for are those who don't have any responsibility. Theodore Roosevelt put it well when he said, "No man needs sympathy because he has to work . . . . Far and away the best prize that life offers is the chance to work hard at work worth doing."

Don't let your children lure you into the trap of self-pity. They do this ever so cunningly, with comments like, "I always do all the work," "I did it last time," "It's not my turn," "None of our friends have to work as much as we do," or "The Parkers are going camping today—why don't we ever do anything fun?" Admittedly, it can be a bit more challenging to get your children to work if the neighbor children are outside playing; but if you're sly about it, you may be able to con the neighbor kids into helping, too. If not, let your children know how grateful you are for their help, and keep telling yourself that you're really doing this for their own good. Someday they may even thank you!

After listening to my presentation on teaching children to work, one mother mentioned that she, too, believed in the importance of work. She went on to say that she had already been teaching her children many of the things that had been discussed; but it was reassuring to know that she was not a mean mother. Then she quickly added, "Or at least I know I'm not the only mean one!"

Childhood, of course, is all about fantasy and imagination. The world is the child's laboratory, filled with intrigue and wonder, ever beckoning to be explored. Naturally, a child should be allowed sufficient time for a thorough investigation and scientific analysis of his surroundings. In other words, there should be plenty of time for carefree romping and creativity. Most children, though, despite what they might tell you, are not lacking adequate play time.

All too often, we focus on the importance of play at the exclusion of work. "They're just children," we say. And, at the risk of being viewed as "mean ogres" we trade momentary pleasure for our children's future happiness and success. We must not short-change them with such short-sighted reasoning. There is sufficient time in our children's lives for both work and play, and they must know that play is something that happens after the work is completed. Play is a privilege to be earned, not a right to be demanded. ". . . [W]hen pleasure or recreation becomes an end in itself, we are in danger. We are in trouble. We simply cannot expect to refine the substance of character from the husks of pleasure."[4]

---

4. *Standing for Something,* Gordon B. Hinckley, Three Rivers Press, New York, NY, 2000, p. 95.

"They Don't Do It My Way"

Principle—There's more than one way to skin a cat.

Is your way the only way? Be willing to relinquish some control. The end result is what is really important. Explain the essentials, and then leave them alone. Children really can be creative. They may find a better way to do things or they may find a way that for them makes the task more enjoyable. Once your children have been sufficiently trained, don't look over their shoulder or stand around nagging or scolding.

One summer I decided it was time to catch up on scrapbooks. Realizing that my teenagers were now old enough to do their own, I solicited their help. Although reluctant at first, they soon caught the spirit of it. I had hoped they would spend at least an hour on the project; but they ended up spending the entire evening at the kitchen table, cutting and gluing, laughing and reminiscing. Not only did they have an enjoyable time, but I was delighted to discover that they had also done an excellent job, adding decorations and captions that I would have considered too time consuming.

Ironing pillowcases. At our house, my children iron the pillowcases. I know . . . I know—ironing is becoming a lost art. A friend has already informed me that pillowcases don't really need to be ironed. And, when I mention the word "iron" to my sister, she gives me a strange, quizzical look and asks, "What is that?" She must know what it is, though, because she keeps an iron as part of her antique collection. Nevertheless, at our house we still iron; and pillowcases are good practice for younger children.

The problem is that my children fold the pillowcases in half lengthwise, then in fourths; I fold them in thirds lengthwise, then in fourths. As you can guess, this creates a problem when stacking them in the linen closet. In the beginning, I tried to get them to do it my way. It was after all, the way I had been doing it for years—and my mother before me. But my way was too hard for the children; and in the end, they did what worked best for them. Finally, in order to keep the stacks of pillowcases from toppling over in the closet, I decided to break with tradition; and *I* began doing it *their* way. I decided that it really didn't matter, and it certainly wasn't worth making into an issue.

Do not misinterpret your children's revelry as detracting from the work. In truth, the merriment actually enhances the work experience. Think back to your most pleasant work experiences. What makes them memorable? Most likely there was some sort of fun associated with them.

I remember shelling peas by the hour as a child. The job itself was tedious and boring, and the days were long and hot. We could have easily lost interest after the first bucketful, but we made it fun by laughing and joking and setting up contests to see who was the fastest or who could shell the most peas. I also remember considerable discussion over who got to tend the baby when he cried. We all adored Steven, but he was never more loved than on those long work days when he provided a welcome diversion from the task at hand. When I reflect on those times now, I don't remember much about the misery of it—that is overshadowed by the memories of the good times I had with my sisters.

I have also noticed my own children sharing meaningful time together at the kitchen sink as they wash dishes. Sometimes they talk about the school day—sharing their frustrations and challenges or relating a funny incident. Sometimes they recite lengthy passages from their favorite movies, the two of them conversing back and forth as if they were the real actors. And, sometimes, my oldest daughter likes to serenade her dishwashing partners with renditions of her favorite songs—much to the chagrin of her dishwashing partner!

Do not create drudgery. The importance of making work enjoyable was reinforced one summer while working in the garden. The first day we weeded, my daughter, who has a get-down-to-business style, suggested that everyone do their own row. That way, everyone could do their fair share and would know when they were finished. This seemed like a reasonable solution, and we each set about doing our work.

The next day, however, my oldest son was home. On this day, the children sat clumped together, sharing the work on just two rows at a time, laughing and talking as they went. Time passed more quickly, and the children hardly noticed they were working. I noticed a difference between the two days; and one of the children commented on the difference, too.

We adults are too serious. We focus too much on bottom lines and end results. And, sometimes we think that our way is the only way or, at least, the best way; and we try to convince our children that because we are the adults, we know best. Too much emphasis is placed on *how* the work is getting done rather than *what* is getting done, and efficiency too often takes precedence over enjoyment. In our hustle-bustle, Day-timer world, we often miss out on the simple pleasures of life by failing to find the fun in what we do.

Children, on the other hand, are very clever at finding ways to turn the most mundane work into some sort of a game. As long as the work is getting done, leave them alone. Finding fulfillment in our work does not necessarily come from doing what we enjoy but rather from learning to enjoy what we have to do. As the years roll by, the misery of the work will be remembered less and less while the companionship and merriment is remembered more and more, unless, of course, there was no merriment—then all that *can* be remembered is the misery.

"My Children Aren't Capable"

Principle—If you think they can or can't, you're right.

You might be surprised at their capacity—I was! At eighteen months, Marissa could set and help clear the table, a two-year-old can rinse and stack dishes, a three-year-old can vacuum, an eight-year-old can mow the lawn, and a fifteen-year-old can prepare an entire meal from scratch.

Out of necessity, we found out just how capable our children were. It was a very busy, very stressful summer. I was in the last trimester of pregnancy with our eighth child and my husband was acting as the general contractor of our new home, which consumed every spare minute. Consequently, this left the children in charge of the outside chores: feeding the chickens, gathering the eggs, feeding and milking the goats twice a day, and bottle feeding the baby goats three or four times a day. They also did all the weeding and watering in the garden and kept me informed of which vegetables were ready for harvesting. I was pleasantly surprised to see how well the children managed with very little supervision. In addition, they had their regular household chores, summer yard work, and our usual canning of fruits and vegetables. They did all of this, by the way, without getting paid for any of it—which is the topic of another section.

Do not underestimate the capacity of your children—even the little ones. They like to please, and they can sense when they're performing "grown up" work and will respond accordingly. Give them a chance; resist the urge to say, "Let me do it," or to shoo them away, saying, "You're too little." This merely reinforces the idea that they aren't capable and trains them to be lazy.

Even when the task really is too difficult for small children, there is usually some part of it they could do. Find something—even if it means more work for you and makes the project take a little longer. There is no magical age when a child suddenly becomes old enough to help. Rather, it is a gradual process that should begin as soon as they show interest in helping, which usually happens shortly after they begin to walk. If you keep telling them they aren't big enough, strong enough, or old enough, then when they really are big enough, strong enough, or old enough, they won't want to help.

Little children love to help. They especially enjoy helping in the kitchen. They love to chop, dice, peel, grate, and stir. When they're "helping," keep in mind two rules of delegation: patience and tolerance. Allow extra time for the task to be completed and plan on things being a bit messy—sometimes a whole lot messy. But, if you have the time and the patience, they really can be quite helpful.

One night I was cutting broccoli for dinner when my two-year-old brought a chair and insisted on "helping." He really was in the way and hindered more than he helped; but I let him rinse the pieces of broccoli and hand them to me anyway. With each succeeding broccoli stem, I sensed his self-esteem growing; and piece by piece, we grew a little closer in those few precious minutes we shared at the kitchen sink. The task may have taken a little longer, but it was well worth it.

A word of caution: Be sure your children know how to properly use the tools, equipment, cleaning supplies, etc., that may be necessary to complete a task. They need to be aware of the dangers involved. My children learn early on how to properly use a knife, and they do very well. However, I was tending the neighbor boy one day who used a knife to cut an apple and ended up cutting off the end of his finger.

Give them a chance. When you're weeding, give them a shovel and let them dig in the dirt or let them pick up the weeds and throw them in the garbage. (I even buy child-size work gloves so they can be just like Mommy.) Let them help dust furniture, mop floors, and bring in groceries. Obviously, they can't carry a full bag of groceries; but they can carry a box of crackers or a package of toilet paper. You will find that they love to show off by carrying as much as possible in order to prove how strong they are. As they grow bigger, they'll be able to carry two or three items; and before you know it, they'll be carrying full bags of groceries right along with the rest of the family.

I found out by accident that my six-year-old could change the sheets on her bed. I was changing the sheets on my son's bed when Jadee asked if she could make her own bed. Instinctively, I thought to myself, "She's too little to make her own bed, but I'll let her try until I'm finished here." Much to my surprise, when I finished with my son's bed, Jadee had finished with hers. Unfortunately for my daughter, she had just proven she could take on an another job; and that became her, and her older brother's, permanent task whenever the sheets were changed.

Don't expect too much. Let your preschoolers do as much as their attention spans allow. They may work for a while, then run off to play. Some days they may surprise you by how intently they will stick with a project, and the very next day they may be completely disinterested. Some days four-year-old Levi fusses and complains when asked to set the table, other days he volunteers to set it. Gradually they will be able to do more and more, working longer periods of time.

Teach them that when the family works, they all work. Even though the little ones may not make a significant contribution, it is important that they attempt to help or at least play nearby. Do not leave them in the house to watch television or play with their toys. They will learn much by watching the family work; and by making even the smallest contribution, they will come to perceive themselves as helpers.

One morning we were all out weeding the flower beds. Four-year-old Levi and eighteen-month-old Melia started out with good intentions. They pulled a few weeds and dug around in the dirt a bit. However, they soon lost interest and spent the rest of the morning wandering around the yard, chasing and playing nearby while the rest of us worked. Levi, however, was anxious to get on with the "business" of the day which included playing with his two older brothers and was tired of waiting for them. Bored and exasperated, he at length declared in a whiney voice, as he strolled across the lawn, "I'm getting tired of working!"

With delegation comes the realization that mistakes will be made. It is important that these mistakes are used as learning experiences and stepping stones to greater achievement. Talk about what went wrong and why. Were you partially to blame? Were the expectations unclear? Was there insufficient training? Is it possible that they really weren't capable of performing the task given to them? Attack the problem without attacking the person. Try to ignore the faults unless they're crucial. *Praise in public, reprove in private.*

There is something to praise in every task, even if it's only the effort itself. One day, three-year-old Caleb came into the kitchen, took me by the hand, and led me to the bathroom. He stood there beaming as he proudly showed off the bathroom sink that he had just "cleaned." To *him* it was a symbol of success— a special surprise that he had undertaken without being asked. To *me,* it looked like a big mess and a lot of extra work. There were puddles of water on the counter and grit all over the sink. At that moment, there were a lot of things I could have said: "What are you doing? You're too little to clean the bathroom sink. Don't get into that stuff unless Mommy helps you. Look what you've done; you've made a big mess, and now I'm going to have to clean it up." Any one of these comments would have burst his little bubble, telling him he had failed. Fortunately, I had my wits about me this day, and instead I said, "That was really nice of you to clean the bathroom sink without being asked. You're such a big boy!"

I didn't need to mention any of the truth that would be detrimental to his self-esteem, nor did I need to say anything that was untrue such as "What a good job you did." He hadn't done a good job. What he had done was create extra work for me, *but* he had done it with good intentions; and the least I could do was praise his noble effort. Because of the sense of achievement gained from cleaning the sink that day, he cleaned it again a few days later—much to my dismay! But I'm a pretty fast learner; and when I realized a pattern was evolving, I decided to help him learn to do it better so he could actually be helpful. I said something to him like: "That's so nice of you to clean the sink. Let me show you a few things." I then proceeded to show him how to rinse the sink, wring out the cloth and wipe off the counter tops. Before long, he could do it very well; and I was grateful I hadn't crushed his first feeble attempts at being helpful.

Everyone has an emotional bank account; make deposits in your children's often. Praise and encouragement can go a long way in helping a child find success in a difficult project. It is amazing what children will willingly and voluntarily do when they feel their efforts are valued and appreciated. Remember, "You catch more flies with honey than you do with vinegar."

When my oldest daughter was three, she straightened the shoes in her brothers' closet without being asked. Then one by one, she brought each family member to see her accomplishment. A few words of praise was all it took for her to do it again and again week after week.

Children are capable of much more than we often give them credit. Provide opportunities for them to prove themselves. Let them prove you wrong!

"My Children Are Too Busy"

Principle—Work expands to fill the time allotted for its completion.

Sure they're busy, but are they busier than you? Do they make wise use of their time? Do they spend too much time watching television, playing computer games, or just goofing off? Do they procrastinate? Do they dawdle? Are they involved in too many things? Can some of the things they're doing be eliminated or consolidated? For your own sanity, you can't afford *not* to give them more jobs.

Admittedly, many children really are very busy. They are involved in sports, church, music, debate, drama, and work; but with a little planning, even busy children can find ways to fit household chores into their schedules as well. At the foundation of family life there are basic household chores that need attention on a daily, weekly, or monthly basis. Regardless of our pressures as adults, we still have lawns to mow, meals to make, and clothes to clean. Children need to understand that whatever else they may be involved in, it is important that their chores are performed in a timely fashion if the family is to function properly. Their busy lives are only going to get busier when they have their own home and family to care for. Now is the time for them to learn skills such as time management, goal setting, and establishing priorities.

Teach them to work faster and smarter. Help them learn to do more than one thing at a time or to plan the sequence of their tasks to make the most efficient use of their time.

Cleaning the bathroom, for example, can take ten minutes or two hours. Obviously, the two-hour job will be (or should be) a much better job, but we do not always have two hours to spend cleaning the bathroom. And, while you would certainly not want everyone doing a ten minute job every time the bathroom was cleaned, a ten minute job is better than no cleaning at all. Not every task needs to be done one hundred percent every time. It is fair—and promotes a lot of goodwill—to allow busy teens to cut corners occasionally. After all, we adults do it from time to time.

Be flexible. There are times when children are particularly busy. Make allowances. Take advantage of those opportunities to do quiet deeds of service—sweeping a floor, making a bed, doing the dishes. That which goes around, comes around; and those little acts of kindness will reap large rewards in your behalf when you are especially busy. After all, that's what being a family is all about—helping each other during times of crisis.

"My Children Complain"

Principle—Complaining is a child's way of testing a parent's resolve.

They're testing you. Like cows put out to pasture, children have a need to see just how far they can push the fences. Naturally, they'll try to get out of as much work as they can; but once they realize you really are serious, they will perform.

Be polite; treat them with respect. Say please and thank you. *Ask* them to do things rather than telling them: "Would you take out the garbage, please?" "Could you please help Johnny brush his teeth?" "Do you think you could set the table?" "I would really appreciate it if . . ." Now, of course, children must understand when you ask them to do something that it is not really a question but merely a polite way of telling them to do something. Do not let them refuse (*Discipline*, 34-42, and *My Children Refuse to Work* 77-80). Be sure to notice the good things they do and take time to thank them.

Include your children in decisions. Let them feel part of the process—make it a team effort. When there are several things that need to be done, I tell the children which chores are available and let them choose one or two they would like to do.

Give them a choice between two jobs. If you merely ask them to do something, the natural response is usually negative: "No, I would rather continue watching TV or playing basketball or riding my bike." However, by giving them a choice between two or more jobs, you shift their thinking from a choice between work and play to a choice between job one and job two: "Would you like to iron pillowcases or fold sheets?" Immediately, they begin the internal process of evaluating which job would be faster, or easier, or more enjoyable; and without even realizing what is happening to them, they agree to one of the choices. It's a simple mind game, but it works quite well! (Occasionally, they will try to outsmart you by choosing "neither." When this happens, I simply say, "That's not an option.")

The other day, my nine-year-old son and I were cleaning up the kitchen after lunch. After washing the dishes, he thought the work finished and was ready to play. I knew asking him to sweep the floor would cause an outburst, so I simply said, "Would you like to sweep the floor or wash the table?" By allowing him the opportunity to choose, the work didn't seem as burdensome. In fact, he washed the table without any complaint, not even realizing that he had just been part of a conspiracy!

It works on little children, too. Lately, when I ask five-year-old Levi to set the table, he has been telling me "no" or putting up a big fuss. The other day when he came into the kitchen, I said, "Levi, do you want to set the cups or the forks?" Instead of thinking that he really didn't want to do either, he was busy thinking about which job he *did* want to do. He chose to set the forks without any fussing at all.

Make it a game. There are dozens of ways to make work more fun. Have races, set the timer to see how fast they can go, pretend to be a garbage truck picking up toys, close your eyes and see how much they can get done. When my boys are in the middle of an intense cowboy and Indian chase, that is not a good time to ask them to get something from the basement. However, if I tell them that I'm sending them on a dangerous mission to a far off dungeon where they need to rescue three cans of tuna, then suddenly the task becomes part of the play and they dash off in daring pursuit. I have heard many heroic tales of dangers encountered in my very own basement while retrieving cans of this and jars of that from my fruit room shelves!

My husband has come up with a sort of diaper-changing game. With two little girls in diapers, he has mercifully offered to help change diapers. And, in true male style, he has also found a way to involve all the older children. (They love it!) When a diaper needs changing, my husband and children do Jung Kim Po (the paper, rock, scissors game) to see who gets to change the diaper. There is always a lot of anxious excitement as they play to find a winner. It has become the game the children dread, but this unpleasant task has been made less miserable by turning it into a game.

Rotating jobs can add variety and make chores less mundane. Variety is the spice of life, and this is never more true than when it comes to chores. At our house, we change housecleaning chores on a weekly basis, but we rotate dishwashing each meal—one child washing, one rinsing, one sweeping, and the rest clearing the table. The next meal, everyone moves up the line—the rinser washes, the sweeper rinses, etc.

When I was growing up, there were four girls. Two of us did all the dishes for a week, then we traded. We did the housecleaning chores for several months, switching when we felt a need to change.

What chores are rotated and how often will vary from family to family. These changes will depend on your children's personalities, their ages, and their capacities. Ask them what they want to do. While some children enjoy change and variety, others may not. Some children, especially young children, need consistency in order to feel secure and learn to do a job well. Be sensitive to your children's individual needs.

When six-year-old Isaac first entered the weekly cleaning schedule with the older children, he was overwhelmed by some of the tasks. Some of them were too hard for him, or so he thought, and the idea of doing something different every week was overwhelming. It was too much to take on all at once. So, rather than causing a lot of frustration for all of us, we simply let him do the same task every week while the other children continued with their weekly rotation. Because he felt competent and comfortable with his assignment, he did it without complaint. This arrangement worked so well, that we used it for two years. Eventually, though, after persistent lobbying from the older children, he joined the regular rotation and did very well.

Offer to trade. Sometimes when the children complain, I offer to trade their work for whatever task I may be doing, which is almost always less appealing; and immediately, the task I have asked them to do doesn't seem so bad after all. Occasionally, though, they do want to trade—mowing the lawn for fixing dinner, washing dishes for bathing the little ones. This can be a welcome change of pace for both of us. Remember, flexibility is the first rule of delegation.

Help them see the bigger picture. Sometimes when my oldest daughter complains about all the work she's done that day, I put my arm around her and teasingly say something like, "Now you know what it's like to be a mom." Or "You think you've got it bad now, just wait until you're a mom." Obviously, our children will never fully appreciate what it means to be a parent until they are parents themselves. Still, we can help put things in perspective for them by discussing what it is like to be an adult: the time pressures and the work that must be done. Perhaps then the work they are asked to do will not seem as difficult in comparison.

Explain at the start of the day what will be expected. Children have plans, too. Even if their plan is to just watch television all day, it is still a plan; and they become irritable when you keep throwing interruptions into their schedules. This frustration can be alleviated if they know up front what is expected of them that day.

At breakfast we may say something like, "Today we need to weed the flowers, water the garden, change the sheets on the beds, do our Saturday work, mend the pasture fence, and fix a dessert for dinner." Discuss any activities the children may have and decide how everything will be accomplished. This will make it easier for the children to incorporate chores into their schedules. By respecting our children's needs, they will be more likely to respect ours; and by knowing ahead of time exactly what will be expected of them, there will be fewer complaints because there will be fewer surprises.

Permanent delegation lessens conflicts and complaints. This is another area where family councils become critically important. They eliminate the need to continually argue over whose turn it is to do a job or whether it's even fair for them to do it at all. If the *who* will do *what* has already been hashed out in family council, there will be no need to continually discuss it every time it needs to be done. Children will already know they have agreed to do certain chores; and, furthermore, they know that everyone else knows!

Permanent delegation also helps children feel a greater degree of ownership for a task. Now it becomes *their* job instead of just a job Mom or Dad has asked them to do. Hopefully, this will motivate them to assume more responsibility and take greater pride in getting it done and doing it well.

During the school year, I don't assign nights for fixing dinner because I would prefer the children were doing homework. Instead, I ask for help from the children who may not be very busy. Consequently, some children get chosen to help more than others, which leads to complaining because of real or perceived inequality. However, during the summer, when everyone has a night to fix dinner, the complaints cease because now the work is more evenly distributed *and* because it has been formally delegated. It now becomes *their* responsibility. They know ahead of time what is expected of them and can plan for it.

When we first got our dairy goats, my husband did all the milking. Before long, however, Trenton learned to milk and was asked to fill in when my husband was running late or had other commitments in the evenings. He usually performed this task under great protest and after much pleading on my part. As he became more competent at milking, we eventually decided he was old enough to do the milking every night; and we explained to him that this would now be his new responsibility. The very next day he did the milking without even being asked—no complaints, no fussing, no pleading, no arguing. I was amazed at the difference permanent delegation had made.

Point out the value of what they have accomplished. When they're finished with a difficult task, ask them how they feel inside. When a child finishes mopping the floor, I may say, "Wow! That looks nice. That floor sure was dirty. How do you feel now that it's clean?" Or, after a long day of canning, I may say, "Look at all those peaches. Think how good they'll taste this winter." By helping them reflect on their sense of achievement and savoring the feeling of a job well done, they will learn to appreciate the work they do.

"My Children Refuse to Work"

Principle—A child's performance is proportionate to a parent's persistence.

If your child is in a complete state of rebellion, the problem may be more extensive than the scope of this book. However, I do have a few suggestions which may be helpful for your typical rejection.

Let them cool down. When a child says he isn't going to do something and storms off angrily, that is not the time to march into his room and demand that he obey. Leave him alone for a while, giving him time to cool off. After a few minutes of pouting, the child will realize how ridiculous he just acted and that you haven't asked him to do anything unreasonable. Interestingly enough, by allowing the child some time and space, he may end up doing the work without any further argument. If he doesn't, go to his room when he's ready to talk about the problem rationally.

I have found that sometimes there are legitimate reasons the child feels resentful about doing what you've asked him to do. Sometimes there are other issues I am not aware of, or things I may have forgotten. Maybe he has a big project due the next day or maybe I've asked him to do something every time he passed through the kitchen while another child has kept a low profile in their bedroom all day. He may justifiably feel that he is being treated unfairly. By talking about it civilly and sympathetically, you may be able to solve the problem without further escalation.

Look at it from their point of view. One day I was feeling stretched to the limit. Not only had it been an unusually busy day, but I was in charge of dinner that evening at the church for twenty girls and their mothers. By the time I got the baby down for a nap, it was mid-afternoon; and I was starting to panic. Realizing there wasn't enough time to get everything done, I asked my oldest daughter for help in mixing up a batch of roll dough. She rebelled emphatically, "NO, I WILL NOT MAKE ROLLS!"

Hurt and surprised by her outburst, I gave her a verbal lashing. I pointed out how busy I was and how selfish and inconsiderate she was being. I ranted about how anything she was doing was certainly not as pressing as being responsible for feeding forty people that evening.

Normally she did not respond so vehemently, and I wondered what had prompted it. When I talked to her about it later, I understood better and even sympathized. She had been trying all day to get a chance to work on a quilt she was making, but she had been hit with a constant barrage of requests to do other things. She, too, was feeling frustrated. She explained that even if I had asked her at the beginning of the day to make rolls, she would have felt differently. She could have included it in her plans and found a way to work it in. But for me to spring it on her at the last minute was the final straw. Remember, children have plans, too.

Turn off the TV . . . and the computer . . . and Nintendo. These are distractions to even the best of workers, and you can help your children stay focused by eliminating as many distractions as possible. You will be amazed at how much better your children work and how much more they can accomplish without other things calling for their attention.

You will also be amazed at how much faster they get their work done if it needs to be done *before* they play and *before* their friends come over. Have you noticed that the work tends to be done more sloppily and more hurriedly if their friends are hanging around waiting to play? Work will be a greater priority if they aren't distracted.

Hold family councils. I cannot stress enough the importance of a non-threatening environment for voicing opinions and frustrations. Truly listen and try to understand from your children's point of view. Evaluate what is working and what is not. It is possible to reach mutually agreeable compromises.

Family councils make the whole delegation process seem more formal and your children will feel more committed if they have agreed to something in the presence of the entire family. Furthermore, the children will take it upon themselves to act as work watchdogs, constantly on the lookout for siblings who are not performing their work as agreed. Peer pressure alone can be a great motivator!

Some children may still refuse. If reminding them of the family council and petitioning their cooperation is not successful, then you may need to increase the consequences. Children must know they are accountable for their delegated tasks and that there will be consequences for failure to perform. These increased consequences may be different for each child. As a parent, you know your child best and you know what will be most effective. You may need to take away certain privileges such as driving the car, playing Nintendo, watching a favorite TV program, riding their bike, skateboarding, or going out with friends. The consequences are unpleasant enough that performing their work becomes more appealing.

Discipline is a balancing act. The tricky part is finding a solution that is firm enough to teach a lesson, yet not so harsh as to create resentment. If you are too lenient or inconsistent with consequences, there will be no motivation to do the work. Most children will naturally take the path of least resistance. However, being too strict creates feelings of bitterness and anger towards parents and work. The answer lies somewhere in the middle.

It's a delicate balance, and you may not always get it just right. That's part of the trial and error. If you tend to be too soft, work on becoming more strict. If you have been too strict, be willing to acknowledge it and apologize if necessary. Children are very forgiving people; and they will forgive more readily if they know that you meant well, that you are sorry for your mistakes, and that you are trying to improve. "Positional power gives the [parent] the right to give orders; however, it's the personal power earned by being considerate to and respectful of others that gives him or her the right to expect those orders to be carried out effectively."[5]

"Some Children Work Better than Others"

Principle—Individuality is acceptable, incompetence is not.

Anyone with more than one child knows how very unique each child is. This individuality shows up in their work as well. Some children are more self-motivated, some are more conscientious, some work better with others, some work better alone, and some need more instruction or praise. The challenge of parenthood is matching the child with the chore. By understanding your children's personalities, you can better tailor the work to fit their individual needs.

My two daughters, for instance, have very different personalities. If I were to ask them to organize their barrettes, ponytails, and hair pieces, the one daughter would do it with precision, separating them into tidy little containers by color, size, style, etc. The other daughter, however, needs more instruction. By knowing this about her, I can give more instruction at the outset, being very specific about how to sort and which containers to use, thus eliminating a lot of frustration in the end because of unmet expectations.

Workers vs. slackers. Often, we work together as a family on projects. It is an excellent way to build family unity. However, care must be taken to ensure that everyone shares the work load. Sometimes the better workers end up carrying the bulk of the work while the lazier ones coast. If you notice this happening, it

---

5. *Delegate,* Harold L. Taylor, Warner Books, New York, New York, 1989, p. 15.

can be easily remedied by assigning the slacker a specific part of the project—a certain part of the room to clean or a portion of the flower bed to weed. This way they cannot rely on others to do their work, and you can inspect what they have done to determine if their work is satisfactory.

Avoid the "oldest child" or "best worker" syndrome. Being the oldest child myself, I can attest to the importance of fair and equal distribution of work. Once when my mother was preparing to leave, she gave me a list of tasks to perform while she was gone. A bit perturbed that she hadn't told any of my three sisters to do a thing, I can remember grumbling, "What are the other girls going to be doing?"

When you leave the house, make a written list of tasks for each child. This way every child has individual assignments for which they can be held individually accountable. It eliminates excuses such as, "I didn't know," or "I forgot." And it also helps prevent the older ones from being too bossy and the little ones from being picked on.

There is a natural tendency to delegate to the oldest child or the best worker (which are very often the same person) simply because they are more capable, more dependable, or more experienced. My seven- and eight-year-old don't do some of the things my oldest children did, out of necessity, when they were four and six years old. This practice, however, strengthens the oldest child's work ethic and self-esteem while neglecting the other children and encouraging their laziness. It can also cause the oldest child to feel overwhelmed and picked on, thus developing feelings of resentment towards parents and siblings. It requires conscious, deliberate effort to ensure that *each child* learns to work.

Let each child specialize in certain tasks. Just as the oldest child shouldn't do all the work, they also shouldn't get all the privileges. Let each child be the first to learn to do something new. By allowing a younger child to be the first to learn to iron or sew or make bread, you create in them a sense of expertise. At our house, twelve-year-old Camille puts the two-year-old to bed at night, Isaac is my carrot peeler, Caleb is an expert at making mashed potatoes, and Jarom and Abram are excellent garbage dumpers. This does not mean, however, that they perform these tasks exclusively. Even though children may develop expertise, cross-training is essential in a family as well as in a business.

No boy or girl jobs. This cross-training applies to gender as well. For myself, growing up in a family of girls, (my only brother was barely eight when I was married) we never knew there was such a thing as "boy and girl" jobs. In addition to our inside chores, we learned to mow the lawn, feed chickens, weed the garden, pick potatoes, and shovel manure; and the same is true of my own daughters today. Likewise, my boys are learning to cook, iron, sew, mop floors, wash dishes, and change diapers. My goal is for each child to be as competent as possible in running a household before leaving home.

"I'm Starting Too Late in Their Lives"

Principle—You <u>can</u> teach an old dog new tricks.

It's never too late to start. In fact, the older your children are, the greater urgency there should be to change before they get any older. Old habits are hard to break but not impossible.

Older children can better understand your needs, time pressures, and commitments. Get together as a family, allowing them opportunities to voice their opinions. Respect their feelings and the demands placed upon them. Make them feel part of the team. Decide on specific jobs for each child and be sure that everyone understands *what* should be done, *how* it should be done, and *when*. Discuss appropriate consequences for failing to keep their end of the bargain.

Obviously, it is easier to get children working if it has been a way of life since they were young. However, with effort, older children can be "persuaded" to work. Don't give up. Start small and gradually add to their responsibilities. With consistent effort, positive results can be achieved.

Don't let them leave home without the benefit of your tutelage in the basics of housekeeping. My husband once worked with a twelve-year-old scout who had never cracked an egg. This young man had precious little time left for training by his parents. You can give your children the edge on life by taking advantage of your children's remaining years at home to pass on some of the tips and tricks you have learned about cooking, cleaning, laundry, home repairs, and yardwork. Being on their own will be challenging enough without starting out at a disadvantage.

"My Teenagers Are Intolerable"

Principle—There's nothing wrong with teenagers that reasoning with them won't aggravate.[6]

We had heard all the horror stories and had received multiple warnings, "Just wait until they're teenagers!" And so it was with anxious dread that we approached our oldest son's thirteenth birthday. But nothing happened. He seemed to glide through the teenage years unaware of the perplexing role he was supposed to be playing. My husband and I looked at each other and said, "What's the big deal?" Then . . . we had more teenagers. And we have now joined with thousands of baffled and befuddled parents for the most tumultuous roller coaster ride of our lives!

Teenagers . . . what a peculiar group—old enough to think they know it all and too young to know they don't. I believe most

---

6. *Children Who Do Too Little,* Patricia H. Sprinkle, Zondervan Publishing House, Grand Rapids, MI, 1996, p. 115.

teenagers don't mean to be obnoxious. Most of them know how to be civil and decent. In fact, they do very well at church and school, with the neighbors and with their peers. It's a power struggle.

Don't back down. Getting your teenager to work may be more difficult, but it is important that you persist *and* insist that they do their share. Don't let their independence and their stubbornness fool you. Deep down inside, they still really need *and want* you to make them mind. They want to know there are limits of what you will and will not tolerate. The same rules of discipline still apply, although the consequences may need to be a little more tough (*My Children Refuse to Work*, 77-80).

Communication is the key. One of the best ways to show that you value your teen's opinion is to seek their advice. As teens become increasingly independent, they want to have a more active role in what goes on around the house. More than ever, they want to feel listened to, appreciated, and respected. That accomplished, they will be much more willing to do their part.

Communication is not only important with regard to work but in all aspects of their lives. My husband and I have been accustomed to making the decisions about family outings. The general pattern has been for us to discuss it between ourselves, then announce our "exciting" plans to the children. This method has backfired on us several times recently. At last it is beginning to sink in that if we want our teenagers to be happy participants, we need to counsel *with* them *before* making plans.

Respect their time. With a new job for my husband, a new baby, and a new-to-us home on three and a half acres, this past summer has been extremely busy. Consequently, I relied on my children heavily. It seemed like I was always asking someone to do something—changing diapers, fixing meals, cleaning up toys, folding laundry. My husband also called from work regularly, asking the children to do various projects in the yard. One day it dawned on me—especially after the roll incident with my daughter—that our children had little time to call their own. At any given moment throughout the day, they may be called upon to do something. The roll incident was the impetus for our weekly planning sessions and for more detailed daily discussions about what we expected them to do each day while allowing them time for personal projects.

Weekly planning sessions. On Sunday evening, we gather as a family to discuss our plans for the week. This is a two-way street. We learn about our children's plans and commitments, and they learn about ours. It is all written down on a calendar that is posted in the kitchen. This way we can make plans for incorporating chores and other projects into our schedules. It has worked well in helping resolve potential conflicts.

Play together. All work and no play makes a teenager grumpy. (Or, should I say, more grumpy?) Interact with your teen in ways other than work. Start traditions: homemade ice-cream, Sunday night popcorn, family read alouds, sports, watching movies together, fishing and hunting, camping and hiking, playing games around the kitchen table. Help them decorate their room. Spend leisure time with them. Laugh with them. Enjoy being with them.

Be their friend. Get to know them as real people. There is nothing a teenager needs more than a true friend. They will do almost anything for a friend. Why not use that to your advantage? As astonishing as it may seem, this can be a great time for parents. I am enjoying my teenagers. At last I have children old enough to carry on intelligent conversations and old enough to be incredibly helpful. If they know you and like you, they will be more willing to work with you and for you.

Love them. Although it doesn't always show on the surface, a teenager, more than at any other age, yearns to be loved, needed, and accepted. The saying, "When they deserve love the least, they need it the most," is especially applicable to teenagers. Love can overcome so many things.

Learn to let go. Teens have lives, too—often very busy lives. They have plans and goals separate from yours. Recognize their need for greater independence. Be willing to let them make more decisions for themselves. Also be willing to let them suffer the consequences of their decisions.

One Sunday I decided to keep most of the children home from church since they were quite sick and had terribly croupy coughs which I didn't think the congregation would appreciate us sharing with them. When my fifteen-year-old son learned about the plan, he was quite put out. He wanted to know why he couldn't stay home, too. He moaned about how unfair it was. When this got him nowhere, he finally agreed to go to *part* of church. However, he informed me that he would be leaving after the first meeting, walking home two and a half miles if that's what it took. This threat did not get the reaction he had hoped for, so then he tried the "I'm feeling sick, too" ploy. This did not work either, and at last I told him to go to his room and think about what he wanted to do.

It wasn't long before he came into the kitchen, completely dressed for church. With an air of confidence, he announced smugly, "*I* have decided that I *want* to go to church. I want to go to *all* of church, too; and I'm *glad* to do it."

What he was really saying is that this was *his* decision and he didn't want to be coerced into doing anything he didn't want to do. I was prepared to let him stay home if it came to that—thankfully it didn't. By allowing him the opportunity to chose, he came around to the right decision on his own and was much happier about it. If you treat your teenagers with respect, viewing them as the adults they are trying to turn into, the results can be miraculous.

"My Children Expect to Get Paid"

Principle—Money cannot buy a strong work ethic.

Why should children get paid for doing basic chores around the house? You don't get paid for the housework you do. I think it is important for children to learn early on that it takes a lot to keep a family running. Making beds, cleaning house, straightening bedrooms, washing dishes, fixing meals, and mowing the lawn are part of being a family. Children should learn to work for the inward satisfaction it brings. They need to work out of a sense of duty towards the family, not for the reward. Our family motto is, "He who works, eats!" Although it is said in jest, the children understand the message.

Sometimes when I ask my children to do something, they respond with, "What will you give me?" or "What do I get?"

To this inquiry, I respond simply, "You get a good feeling in your heart."

It is important for children to recognize and appreciate the good feeling that comes from serving others. They should learn that sometimes we do things just because they need to be done, with no thought of personal gain.

It doesn't hurt to reward them occasionally—a trip to the library, making cookies, a sleepover, a movie. If we have a hot, miserable job to do, I may say, "Let's hurry and get this done, then we'll have a popsicle." Or, if we have an especially busy Saturday, we can make it more tolerable by promising to make homemade ice cream at the end of the day. Rewards can help take the drudgery out of work and can motivate children to work faster or better, but they should be offered infrequently to be most effective. They must be the exception, not the rule, in order that children do not come to rely on them.

It is a false notion that bribery is the only way to get children to work. Children, especially little children, enjoy helping.

They want to be a part of everything you're doing. By capitaliz-
ing on their innate curiosity and willingness to help when they're
young, they will grow up being naturally helpful.

> It is a myth that children don't want to work. Most children
> love to work and often offer to help. . . .[W]e can reject the
> popular idea that children must be prodded, enticed, or sup-
> plied with any external motivation to participate in family
> chores.
>
> When we speak of motivating others, we accept a nearly
> universal belief among social scientists that all action begins
> with the self. Supposedly, a person's need . . . or their desires
> . . . prompt them to act in their own interest. In theory, then,
> the way to alter another person's behavior is to appeal to that
> self-interest by dangling rewards in front of them. . . .
>
> When we train children to work by paying them, whether
> with money or privileges, we reinforce self-interest. While this
> approach may have positive results in the short term, it often
> disintegrates into manipulative attempts by both parent and
> child to outmaneuver one another.[7]

**The decision, of course, to give your children an
allowance, is a personal one.** But your children would be better
off in the long run if you resist the temptation to tie allowances
to their daily chores. If children need extra money, find something for them to do above and beyond the normal household
tasks.

Better yet, let someone else pay them. Help them find other
ways to make money—a paper route, mowing lawns and doing
yard work for the neighbors, babysitting, walking dogs, shoveling snow, raking leaves. There are dozens of entrepreneurial
ideas for the creative and the ambitious.

Before moving to Hawaii, my four oldest children shared
three paper routes. They bought their own bikes and roller

blades. Because they used their own hard-earned money, their purchases meant more and they took better care of them.

When I was young, Dad cut up our surplus banana squash, weighed it, priced it, and put it in a wagon. We children went door-to-door, selling it to the neighbors. We thought it was great to be able to earn our own money.

This past year our family ended up with thirty bushels of apples from our five apple trees. We sorted them into small bags; and our four youngest boys, ages five to ten, set out to sell them to the neighbors. This was no small undertaking. The blocks in our neighborhood are one-half mile long, making it a two-mile walk around one block. Because of the distance involved, I had expected my boys to go to a few close neighbors on our street. However, they surprised me with their perseverance. They spent all afternoon walking the "neighborhood", coming home part way through the afternoon just long enough to drop off the five-year-old who was getting tired, get a drink of water, and pick up more apples. By the time they finished, they had spent more than five hours peddling apples and walked nearly five miles. It's amazing what children will do when motivated to make money.

Instead of using monetary rewards as motivators, try positive reinforcement. Sometimes the best payment of all is a loving pat on the back, a few words of praise, or a genuine thank you—verbal or written. We all like to be thanked for our efforts. I know for myself, it's nice to be told "thank you" for those daily tasks that mothers are "supposed" to do. I wash and iron my husband's clothes every week, but it sure makes the effort seem more worthwhile when he notices what has been done and takes the time to thank me. Thank your children occasionally for the chores they are "supposed" to do. Notice when they do a little extra or when they do a job especially well.

Ideally, a little recognition is all the payment children should need. However, sometimes it takes a little more to get them started initially. For example, from time to time I have trouble getting the little ones to make their beds, brush their teeth, get dressed, and comb their hair in the morning. I could spend the morning nagging and scolding or I could inflict some sort of punishment, but I have found that a little positive motivation works much better. Setting the timer for fifteen minutes, I tell them that whoever is all ready when the timer rings gets to pick a treat. At first they want the treat immediately, but after a few days they forget to ask for it until 20-30 minutes later, then an hour, and then maybe half a day; and before too long, they no longer need the candy at all. All they really needed was a little help in forming a habit. This same kind of motivation works well with homework, practicing the piano, or any chore that seems especially difficult or demanding.

Brag about your children. Brag to others about the good things your children do *when they're around*. It is fun to watch their faces light up as they beam with pride while trying to look embarrassed. Make it a point to mention to grandma or the neighbor that your seven-year-old can now mop floors, your five-year-old cleaned the bathroom sink today, or your three-year-old is learning to make his own bed. When we have company for dinner, I make sure to mention the part each child has played in the preparation of the meal. A little public recognition goes a long way in bolstering self-esteem and making children want to perform even better the next time. As someone has summed it up best, "A child may not always remember what you say, but he will always remember how you made him feel."

Too much praise can be harmful. Be careful when praising, thanking, or bragging about your children. Don't overdo it. If done too frequently or excessively, it can be harmful. Avoid using excess flattery or being too gushy. These techniques are similar to working for pay, and children learn to work for external recognition rather than their own internal sense of accomplishment. An occasional, sincere, heartfelt compliment is much better.

Other incentives. When I notice that a child has done an exceptional job or has been especially helpful, I tape a little note to their bedroom door in recognition of their effort. These are made out of colorful paper and displayed for all to see. They may earn one of several awards which are represented by corresponding pictures:

• **Busy Bee**—doing something that is especially hard or time consuming

• **Helping Hand**—helping out more than usual, especially without being asked

• **X-tra Miler**—going above or beyond what was asked

• **Happy Helper**—cheerful attitude, saying, "sure" or "I would be glad to."

On the award, I write the child's name and what they have done. Not only is this a fun way of saying thank you, but it also gives them a little public recognition for those extra efforts that often go unnoticed. And, hopefully, this subtle motivation will inspire everyone to try a little harder.

I realized these awards were having some impact when I overheard my five-year-old explaining to one of his friends about the "X-tra Miler" award that was taped to his bedroom door. And while I'm sure the little friend had no idea what my son was talking about, it struck me how much this simple bit of recognition meant to my child.

Chore charts. I know many people like to use chore charts and stickers or some other incentive. I have seen some pretty creative charts, and I think there is some merit in this approach. Colorful charts are certainly appealing to children; and they can be helpful initially, especially with younger children, in getting them used to the idea of doing chores and having daily tasks.

Charts are also effective as reminders of who should do what. Our "chart" consists of a little 3x5 piece of paper on the corkboard in the kitchen listing Saturday chores. If a child forgets what he should do, a quick check of the "chart" will remind him.

However, the drawback to charts and incentives is that it is one more project to keep up with. They also tend to have only short-term effects. If the motivation to work comes from the sticker or the chart, then as the newness and excitement wears off, you find yourself with the added burden of continually making new charts and coming up with clever incentives to keep your children working.

Getting your child to work is not unlike potty training. Initially, with potty training, we bribe the child with treats every time he uses the bathroom; but as the child establishes a routine, the treats gradually become less and less while the expectation remains the same. So it is with work—the long-term goal is for children to do what needs to be done simply because it needs to be done. It is absurd to think that we would give our sixteen-year-old a treat every time he used the bathroom. And, yet, we often treat our teenagers like two-year-olds when it comes to work. The motivation and the reward for work should come from a child's own inward feeling of accomplishment. Eventually, that is where all motivation must come from anyway.

4
REWARDS OF DELEGATION

*Only those who do not know how to work do
not love it.—.J.H.Patterson*

By now, I hope it is obvious that there are many rewards for delegating. By way of summary and as a last-ditch effort to convince you, if you are not already convinced, I will explain the benefits here.

- Saves your sanity
- Creates more free time
- Enhances children's self-esteem
- Keeps children busy
- Promotes Greater family unity
- Teaches children the value of work
- Prepares children for the real world

Saves Your Sanity

Whether you have a full-time or part-time career or are a full-time homemaker, whether you are married or a single parent, and whether you have two children or a houseful, I think you would agree there is too much to do and too little time in which to do it. All too often we try to be "superdad" or "supermom," but reality dictates that we simply cannot and should not do it all. Children create the majority of our work, so it is only reasonable that they should do their part to help.

Do not play the martyr. Parenthood is stressful enough without taking on more than necessary. For the sake of our physical, mental, and emotional well being, we *must* delegate. In fact, our sanity depends upon it!

Sometimes it is next to impossible to get things done without our children's help. For example, when our family has church at 8:00 a.m., there is no way we could make it on time without delegating to the older children. Each Sunday morning while eating breakfast, various tasks are delegated: one child will prepare the diaper bag; each of the older children will help a younger child get dressed, comb their hair, and brush their teeth; someone else will scrub potatoes; and someone else will do the dishes . . . then I calmly stroll to the bathroom to do my hair!

My children rescue me from an embarrassing moment. It was two days before Christmas, and I had a mother/daughter dinner that evening with my oldest daughter. As I was in charge of making all the lasagna for the meal, I got started early in the morning.

At noon, my daughter informed me that she absolutely *had* to have something from town (an hour away); and the next day being Christmas Eve, the store would not be open. Since the lasagna was already made, I figured we could run to town and back and still have time to get ready for the dinner.

Of course, the trip took longer than expected; and on the way home, I broke into a cold sweat, realizing that we would not be home in time to cook the lasagna. This was one meeting for which I could not be late! Stopping at a pay phone (I know. This is the twenty-first century, and they do make cell phones), I called home to ask my son if he could get the lasagna baking, which involved cooking some of it in the neighbor's oven. I also asked him to make some salad dressing for that evening.

Then I drove on, feeling confident that things were now under control. But alas, as I continued to drive, I remembered more details that had not been taken care of. Again, I started to panic and pulled over once more to call home, asking the children to do several more things. (What a ridiculous idea to go to town on a day like this. What was I thinking?)

We arrived home just in time to change clothes, throw everything in the van, and take off again. Thanks to my children having everything ready, I was spared what could have been a terribly embarrassing moment.

Again they saved the day. On another long shopping trip (every shopping trip was long in Hawaii), I called home to tell the children I was running late and to give them a few instructions about dinner. Since I knew I would be home just in time to put them to bed, I also asked if they could bathe the little boys. I was surprised and touched to hear my son say, "It's already been done, Mom."

These are the paydays of delegation. Obviously, they don't happen every day. Just like the business world, there is an awful lot of stress and effort and time and energy and plain hard work between paychecks. And sometimes the payments from your children are few and far between, but when payday finally comes, you will know that all the effort has been worthwhile.

Creates More Free Time

By delegating many of your routine tasks, you will have more time to work on other projects, help children with homework, manage the household, develop skills or talents, or pursue personal goals. If I can get one or more of the children to fix dinner, I may have an extra half hour for exercising, sewing, gardening, or writing this book.

From our library window where I am typing, I can see several children in the backyard. The younger ones are picking up apples and branches that have fallen off the trees so the lawn can be mowed, another child is mowing the lawn, and still another is sweeping the patio. Saturday chores have already been done, and my husband is planning to make a Dutch oven dinner so I won't have to cook. Which means, of course, that several of the children will be in the kitchen helping him . . .

This book could have never been written without the help of my entire family. My husband has generously volunteered to tend children, cook meals, clean house, run errands, and change diapers so I could have time for writing. He and the children have even spent Saturday afternoons making salsa and applesauce while I typed at the computer. Likewise, each of the children has gone the extra mile in helping babysit, do laundry, take care of the garden, and fix meals. It has definitely been a group effort.

I never cease to be amazed at what can be accomplished when the family works together. Housework, yard work, cleaning the garage, organizing the basement, canning, or any other project goes faster when everyone helps. Then, instead of the parents spending the day working while the children play, everyone can have some free time. As I have said, many hands make light work.

Parenthood is synonymous with sacrifice. Being a parent often means giving up some of our own personal goals, ambitions, and dreams—or, at least, putting them on hold for a while. However, it doesn't mean giving up everything. Reward yourself with some "me" time occasionally. Doing something that is personally rewarding or fulfilling is not a selfish thing. It doesn't hurt the children at all to fix dinner while you exercise or to tend the baby while you nap. (As grumpy as I get when I'm sleep deprived, the nap is as much for the children as it is for me!)

Don't feel guilty. Taking time for you is actually a benefit to your children. Your children learn valuable lessons on work, service, and being unselfish. You, in turn, give them the gift of a happier, more patient parent.

Enhances Children's Self-Esteem

Children really do want to please, and they crave attention. One of the most meaningful ways to do this is to give them responsibility. Although they may fuss and complain and try to get out of work, their self-esteem will grow as they begin to feel they are making a significant contribution to the family.

Most children, even very small children, like to feel productive and important. When my son, Jarom, was five, he became interested in helping in the kitchen. Each night as dinner was being prepared, he bounded into the kitchen to ask what he could do to help. Each night I gave him the same answer, "You can set the table." With a family as large as ours, this was a very helpful thing to do. He apparently did not share my sentiments. After several nights of cheerfully setting the table, he came into the kitchen and again asked what he could do to help. Before I could respond, however, he quickly added, "And don't say set the table. I want to do something *important.*"

I am reminded of a Wheaties commercial on television years ago when I was a child. I don't remember all the details, but my closest recollection is of a father and son sailing on the ocean. The sun is just peeking over the horizon; and naturally, they are eating Wheaties for breakfast. As the fathers turns the steering of the vessel over to his teenage son who, with a look of surprise and smug assurance, takes control, a voice in the background declares, "Wheaties . . . when a boy finally knows he's a man."

The tasks we assign our children tell them our perceptions of themselves. We can do much to raise their self-esteem by giving them assignments that imply trust and approval. Provide opportunities for them to do things at the limit of their capacity. Where there is no challenge, there is no growth.

Recently, I watched in frustration as two-year-old Melia struggled to fasten her snaps. I thought it was a hopeless cause, but she insisted on doing it herself. When she was at last successful, she looked at me and exclaimed triumphantly, "Did it, Mom!"

While your ten- or twelve-year-old may not be quite as enthusiastic about her chores, the feelings inside are just as real. The next time she does a particularly difficult task or she does something especially well, notice the gleam in her eye and the look of pride and satisfaction on her face. She even seems to act a little older and stand a little taller as if to say, "It was hard, but I did it!"

Keeps Children Busy

Too many children spend too much time watching television, playing computer games, sleeping in, and hanging out with friends. Statements such as "There's nothing to do," "I'm bored," "I can't wait for school to start," are reflective of their excess leisure time. Too much free time is a recent phenomenon unknown to children of earlier generations.

Excess leisure and the resulting boredom is fast becoming a national epidemic. It manifests itself in society's escalating dilemma with gangs, violence, and vandalism. Idle minds are the devil's workshop; G.C. Lichtenberg noted that "the greater part of human misery is caused by indolence."

On a smaller scale, boredom in the home leads to fighting and teasing and mischief. It creates a general feeling of unrest. Many of our problems at home and in our communities could be dramatically reduced if parents kept their children busy with work and other productive, meaningful activities.

Most children do not naturally look for productive ways to spend their time. The tendency is to choose the path of least resistance. Therefore, it may take some effort and encouragement on your part to motivate them, but the rewards will be worth it. There are so many worthwhile things they could be doing: sewing, fixing meals, baking bread, drawing, reading,

painting, growing a garden, learning a trade or a musical instrument, or starting a home business. Be creative. The possibilities
are limited only by your own imagination.

Promotes Greater Family Unity

My four boys, ages four to ten, were doing outside chores the
other day—feeding and watering the animals and gathering
eggs. Since the weather had just turned cold, they were excited-
ly running back and forth to the kitchen sink, filling jugs with hot
water for the animals. After several trips to the sink, I heard six-
year-old Abram remark, "We're a team!"

Teamwork is a term generally associated with sports and ath-
letic events, but it has application to families as well. By working as a team, victory is achieved on the baseball field, the
basketball court, and the hockey rink. Likewise, success and
unity in the family is realized when individual members work
together toward common goals.

By working together, children learn important social skills
while simultaneously developing bonds of friendship, as reflect-
ed in the following testimonials of college students:

> I never realized why my older brother and I were such good
> friends. When we were in our early teens, we helped my dad
> build our house, install the sprinklers, landscape the yard, and
> do all sorts of odds-and-ends jobs. I remember many times
> when we would have to cooperate to accomplish many of our
> work goals. . . . Now that we are older, there is a bond that we
> share because we worked side by side in our developing years.
> I would not trade them for anything.[1]

---

1. "The Sacred Nature of Everyday Work," Meridian, Kathleen
Slaugh Bahr, pp. 4, 5.
    (http://www.ldsworld.com/ldsworld/print/1,2143,everydaywork+li
brary,00.html)

When I was in the 4th grade, my mom started a bakery business selling breads and cinnamon rolls to bring in some extra money. . . . As children, it was our job to wash the containers everyday. . . . We dreaded [it] but we did it anyway. I remember laughing so hard on some days, and I remember being so mad at my brother on other days that I knew I could never forgive him (until two minutes later when he would do something that would be so funny and make me laugh). . . . I've always felt especially close to my brother, and I have believed for a long time that it is because we had to work and spend so much time together while growing up.[2]

One study concludes that children who work with and for family members learn to be less self-centered and more focused on the needs of the family a whole:

Canadian scholars . . . compared children who did "self-care tasks" such as cleaning up their own rooms or doing their own laundry, with children who participated in "family-care tasks" such as setting the table or cleaning up a space that is shared with others. They found that it is the work one does "for others" that leads to the development of concern for others, while "work that focuses on what is one's "own," does not. . . . In one international study, African children who did "predominantly family-care tasks [such as] fetching wood or water, looking after siblings, running errands for parents" showed a high degree of helpfulness while "children in the Northeast United States, whose primary task in the household was to clean their own room, were the least helpful of all the children in the six cultures that were studied.[3]

2. "The Sacred Nature of Everyday Work, Part 3," Meridian, Kathleen Slaugh Bahr, p. 9.

3. World Congress of Families II, Kathleen Slaugh Bahr, Geneva, Nov. 14-17, 1999, p. 6 (http://www.worldcongress.org/gen99/speakers/gen99/bahr.htm)

"Doing nothing for others is the undoing of ourselves" (Horace Mann). Work is not just about getting the chores done more quickly. Through work, children learn valuable lessons on service and sacrifice. In a very practical way, they learn to share; and in so doing, they become less concerned about "me" and more concerned about "we". By giving of themselves for the benefit of others, they become less selfish and less demanding. Working with and for others, not only strengthens friendships; but it also develops greater love and concern for them. After all, we learn to love those we serve.

Autumn is my favorite time of year. It's more than the cool, crisp air; the colored leaves; and the smell of fresh-cut hay. Fall is the season of triumph: lush, green plants with mature fruit; cornstalks and melons and pumpkins standing in the fields; vine-ripened tomatoes and juicy apples right off the tree. At last all the work and efforts of the past several months begin to pay off.

It has been fun to see my children's excitement over our garden last year. Since we didn't plant a garden the three years we lived in Hawaii, my younger boys didn't remember what it was like to grow our own food. The whole garden experience—from tilling the ground in springtime to planting and watering the little seeds and watching them sprout to harvest time was a thrilling adventure.

They kept me informed all summer on the progress of the garden: the ripening of the tomatoes and each new melon and pumpkin on the vine. There was great excitement over our first ears of corn, our first zuchinni, and, of course, the long-awaited, much anticipated event of picking our first watermelon—not a day too early nor a day too late. When we walked through the garden, there was a sense of comradeship and accomplishment that was indescribable. It was not a fleeting, momentary pleasure, but rather an enduring sense of achievement from days and weeks of laboring together.

Again, let me emphasize that farming is not the only way to build family unity. When we built a new home a few years ago, it was a family project: putting on the roof, laying a wood floor, setting tile, sanding and staining, and sweeping and sweeping and sweeping. The children threatened to mutiny if they had to sweep one more time! But when we finished, it was *our* house. Similarly, the house we now own has required some fix up. Through painting and plumbing, building and remodeling, family unity has increased. Involve your children in whatever it is you do.

Work as a family often. Work is always more enjoyable if Mom and Dad are there, too. Sing songs, listen to music, tell jokes, laugh . . . enjoy being together. Your attitude towards work will rub off on your children, and these family work/play times will become cherished memories that will last a lifetime.

Teaches Children the Value of Work

A century ago, farming was the predominant occupation and the survival of the family depended upon the cooperation of every member. Children learned to work out of necessity. Work came naturally to them, and they did not feel picked on or abused.

While farm life naturally lends itself to the creation of work, it is not essential to the work experience. Perhaps you know a plumber, an electrician, or a carpenter who would be willing to teach your children the skills of his trade. Today, living in crowded subdivisions or high-rise apartment buildings, it takes greater effort on the part of parents to create work for our children; but it can still be done. Look carefully at your surroundings. You may be surprised at how much your children can learn in whatever situation you may find yourself.

Even if you're renting, there are things you can do to teach your children to work. Think of it as your place. Fix it up. Keep it clean. Care for the yard. Grow a garden if possible.

We rented for many years before purchasing our first home. In several of the places we lived, we were able to have a small garden. We always considered it a blessing to be able to work for some of our food and to supplement the grocery budget with fresh, homegrown vegetables. We also kept the lawn mowed, planted flowers, hung pictures, and made curtains. We took pride in our surroundings even though we didn't own them. In the process, we gained a measure of self-respect while providing valuable work opportunities for our children.

If you don't have a yard, there are many things to learn inside the home. Children can learn cooking, cleaning, mending, home repairs, remodeling, painting, and budgeting. They can learn to run the washing machine, iron a shirt, clean an oven, defrost a freezer and unclog a drain. Someday they will be on their own, and suddenly they will be expected to do all these things themselves. They will be better prepared to handle emergencies and the day-to-day stresses of life if much of their daily routine was already second nature. The more tasks children master, the easier adulthood will be.

An excellent place to start is with children's own bedrooms. If children get into the habit of making their beds, picking up their toys, and putting their clothes away on a daily basis, they will not find it too difficult to keep their rooms reasonably clean. They can learn much about tidiness and organization by caring for their personal belongings. And, the effects of cleaning their own rooms will naturally spill over to other parts of the house, making it easier to one day care for their own homes.

An added bonus to children cleaning house is that they are more apt to keep it clean. They will also help other family members keep it clean, too. Who is the first one to get upset when someone dirties the freshly-mopped kitchen floor? The one who cleaned it, of course. When a child has just invested a considerable amount of time and energy cleaning part of the house, he feels a certain degree of ownership over that area; and he will be the first to announce to the family that nobody better get it dirty!

"Children who are taught to work and to enjoy the fruits of that labor have a great advantage as they grow toward maturity. The process of stretching our minds and utilizing the skills of our hands lifts us from the stagnation of mediocrity."[4]

Prepares Children for the Real World

In sharp contrast to childhood, adulthood is all about work. The better children learn to work during childhood, the easier life will be for them as adults. Someday your children will grow up and out of your home and will have to face the real world. They will be much better prepared for that day if they have learned the value of hard work, commitment, sacrifice, and the law of the harvest.

"It is better to build boys than to repair men."[5] The philosophy, "Give a man a fish, you feed him for a day; teach him how to fish and you feed him for a lifetime," applies equally to children and work. Clean your children's rooms and they are clean for a day (if you're lucky!); teach them to clean their own rooms and they can be clean everyday.

"We teach by habit, we teach by precept, and we teach by example. Aristotle says that habituation at an early age makes more than a little difference; it can make almost all the difference. So if you want kids to learn what work is, you should have them work. If you want them to learn what responsibility means, you should hold them responsible. If you want them to learn

---

4. *Standing for Something,* Gordon B. Hinckley, Three Rivers Press, New York, NY, 2000, p. 94

5. *Richard Evans' Quote Book,* Richard L. Evans, Salt Lake City, UT, 9th Printing, 1980, p. 62.

what perseverance is, you should encourage them to persevere. And you should start as early as possible."[6]

By giving our children adult responsibilities, we won't end up with adults who still act like children. Our job as parents is to raise competent, capable, contributing members of society. This process begins today. It occurs bit by bit as we provide opportunities for learning and growth for our children. We do our children no favors by pampering and catering to them.

---

6. "Teaching the Virtues," *Imprimis*, William J. Bennett, Feb. 2003, p. 2. Reprinted by permission from *Imprimis, The National Speech Digest of Hillsdale College*, www.hillsdale.edu.

5

CONCLUSION

The sleep of a laboring man is sweet. —
Ecclesiastes 5:12

Well, we've covered a lot of information. We have outlined the basic rules and principles of delegation and potential stumbling blocks to success. Hopefully, you are now armed with ammunition to combat the stumbling blocks you may encounter in the daily battle of getting children to do their work.

The implementation of delegation will be unique to each family in their varying circumstances. Some families are large, some are small. Some have young children, some have teenagers, and some have a combination of both. The needs of the mother and the capacity of her children also vary widely from family to family. And, as the family grows, so will the capacity and responsibilities of the children.

What works with one child, may not work with another. What worked in our home ten years ago when our two little children began working no longer works with a houseful of children. What works in the summer, doesn't work during the school year. And what works for us now will no longer work when we add another child to the dishwashing rotation or when some of the children have jobs or begin to leave home.

Each aspect of delegation is delicately intertwined, each dependent upon the other for maximum success. And, while the underlying rules and principles remain fixed, there is the never-ending, ever-changing, constantly-evolving process of applying those principles in our individual families.

106

Delegation is not easy, but, then, nothing truly worthwhile usually is. It involves a great deal of energy, and at times you, too, will wonder if it is worth the effort. I can promise you that it is, but you must personally be convinced of that in order to put forth the necessary effort on a daily basis. I hope I have provided some convincing evidence.

Delegation has made it possible for me to do homeschool, keep up with the housework, and write this book, while raising ten children and somehow managing to maintain marginal sanity. **It has boosted my children's self-esteem by giving them a sense of self-worth and belonging while simultaneously teaching them important life skills that will assist them in their ascent to adulthood.**

Many times my children have literally saved the day when something unexpected has come up or when I just had more than I could handle. Even more frequent are their simple, spontaneous acts of service (sometimes performed anonymously): changing a diaper, bathing the little ones, making a bed, folding clothes, fixing a meal, cleaning a cupboard. I can honestly say that I could not do all that I do without the help of my entire family. **Through delegation, we have experienced the effects of synergy, which means that the whole is greater than the sum of the individual members.** Or, in more simple terms, it means we can accomplish twice as much in half the time.

In today's fast-paced, hectic world we seem to be continually searching for those elusive ingredients necessary for strengthening family ties. Society tells us they are found in high-adventure, action-packed, expensive thrills; but we may be surprised to learn that much of what we are seeking can be found within the walls of our very own homes. Too often we hurry through the chores in order to get on with our family fun; and, ironically, in the process, miss out on priceless opportunities to bolster family unity. **Working together can develop a love and**

closeness that can be achieved in no other way. Through our labors, we build character, strengthen friendships, and create enduring memories. In our efforts to fortify family relationships, we must not overlook the remarkable binding power of quietly—or not so quietly—working side-by-side performing the simple, ordinary, daily tasks of life.

APPENDIX

When I'm not working, I get tired of myself. —Herbert Hoover

Summary of Stumbling Blocks and Principles

I can do it faster myself—*The best investment you can give your child is your time.*

If you want it done right, do it yourself—*You get what you expect.*

I find it enjoyable—*If you keep all the plums for yourself, the only thing left for others is the pits.*

I'm a creature of habit—*If you always do what you've always done, you'll always get what you've always got.*

I'm not organized enough—*The more you delegate, the more time you have to organize; and the more organized you become, the easier it becomes to delegate.*

I feel sorry for them—*Hard work never killed a man, but it sure has scared a lot of them.*

They don't do it my way—*There's more than one way to skin a cat.*

I'm starting too late in their lives—*You <u>can</u> teach an old dog new tricks.*

My children aren't capable—*If you think they can or can't, you're right.*

My children are too busy—*Work expands to fill the time allotted for its completion.*

My children complain—*Complaining is a child's way of testing a parent's resolve.*

Some children work better than others—*Individuality is acceptable, incompetence is not.*

My children refuse to work—*A child's performance is proportionate to a parent's persistence.*

My teenagers are intolerable—*There's nothing wrong with teenagers that reasoning with them won't aggravate.*

My children expect to get paid—*Money cannot buy a strong work ethic.*

Children's Chores Based on Age

The following lists will serve as guides for chores children are capable of performing with little or no supervision at various ages. Obviously, an older child should be able to do everything listed for a younger child. As mentioned in the book, the abilities of children to perform tasks will vary from child to child and from family to family.

18 months – 2 years

set/clear table   pick up toys
put clothes in drawer

3 years

rinse dishes   load dishwasher
entertain baby   straighten shoes in closet
dress and undress themselves

4 – 5 years

empty garbage
sort socks
bring in groceries
sweep

make bed
fold underwear
dust
simple vacuuming

6 – 7 years

clean bathroom sink
dress younger children
grate cheese
shovel snow
iron pillowcases
sweep patio
change sheets

scrub toilets
chop food—handle a knife
rake leaves
feed baby a bottle
feed/water inside animals
help with canning

8 – 9 years

feed/water outside animals
mow lawn
fix simple meals
clean bathtub
load washer and dryer
change diapers
straighten clothes drawers

wash dishes
tend siblings
mop floors
vacuum
water outside plants
wash walls
weed garden and flowers

10 – 11 years

hang clothes on outside line
shovel more snow
wash windows

follow recipes
bathe younger children
sort laundry

12 years

simple mending   sewing
iron clothes   babysitting
fix complete meals

Teenagers

operate equipment:

   chain saw   bake from scratch

   weed eater   defrost freezer

   tiller   clean oven

   power tools   home repairs

clean refrigerator   make bread

edge lawn   change oil in vehicles

INDEX

113

ABOUT THE AUTHOR

Debbie Bowen is a full-time homemaker and mother of ten children, six boys and four girls. Her experience and expertise for writing this book has been gained from the day-to-day, real life struggles of raising her own children. She has given numerous workshops on the topic of delegation and teaching children the value of work.

In addition to writing, she enjoys sewing, gardening, trying new recipes, and making flower arrangements. One of the things she most looks forward to is her weekly date with her husband, giving her a chance to unwind and giving the children yet another opportunity to practice the principles outlined in this book.

Debbie's husband works as an administrator in higher education; and as a result of his employment, they spent three years living in Hawaii. It was a wonderful cultural experience for the entire family. However, they have since moved to the little farming community of Hooper, Utah, where their children keep busy taking care of their 3 1/2 acre hobby farm. They describe this change of residence as moving from one paradise to another!